The Wheat Allergy Handbook

The Wheat Allergy Handbook

A step-by-step guide to tests, treatments, safety, travel and more

Goldie Putrym

Harding & Leslie Ltd

Book cover design by printok

Published by Harding & Leslie Ltd

DISCLAIMER

This book is not intended as a substitute for medical advice. It is for general information purposes only. The statements made are not intended to diagnose, treat, cure, or prevent any condition or disease. The author is not a (or the reader's) healthcare provider. The reader must consult with their own physician or healthcare specialist regarding the suggestions and recommendations made in this book.

Although the author and publisher have made every effort to ensure that the information in this book was correct at press time and, while this book is designed to provide accurate information in regard to the subject matter covered, the author and publisher assume no responsibility for errors, inaccuracies, omissions, or any other inconsistencies herein and hereby disclaim any liability to any party for any loss, damage, or disruption caused by errors or omissions, whether such errors or omissions result from negligence, accident, or any other cause. The author and publisher are not liable or responsible for any advice, course of treatment, diagnosis resulting from the use of this book.

This book provides content related to physical and/or mental health issues. As such, use of this book implies your acceptance of this disclaimer.

For S.A. and A.S.

You are my reason

TABLE OF CONTENTS

PREFACE

What stands in the way becomes the way.
-- Marcus Aurelius, Stoic philosopher, Emperor of Rome 161-180

Our first vacation as a family was going fairly well. We were at a resort in the Dominican Republic. Sun, sand, sea, and a stroller. We hadn't visited the swimming pools or the beach once, but at least it was a break from the snow at home and the constant focus on our baby's endless eczema-care routine.

The food options were diverse at the resort with two buffets and eight restaurants on offer. We decided to try out the Mexican restaurant that evening but once we arrived, there was a long wait for a table. Baby was getting very fussy, very fast. Even when we were seated nothing would soothe her. Nursing, rocking, toys – *nada*. She kept trying to reach for my bread roll.

I had decided before the trip that we would not be introducing any new foods while away from home but eventually, at my wits end and with a stomach bug brewing, I gave in and handed the bread to her. Barely seven months old, she only had a few teeth and just managed a tiny nibble before getting bored of it. The whining and crying resumed in full force. I gave up and went back to our room with her.

Back in the hotel room, I tried to get her more comfortable and while trying to nurse her – yet again – I noticed a few mosquito bites on the side of her neck. Then I saw them on the other side. And on her stomach and her back. These were not mosquito bites. They were hives. She was having an allergic reaction!

1

By the time we got to the hospital, she was so swollen that her chin looked like it connected straight onto her chest. No neck in sight. I used all the Spanish I could remember to explain the events to the doctor and several hours and injections later we were back 'safely' at our hotel, except we no longer felt safe. Food nearly killed our baby.

Chances are if you've picked up this book, you know this feeling.

With all the fanfare given to peanut and tree nut allergies, you could be forgiven for thinking – like we did at the time – that they are the only serious ones. Not so. It turned out my daughter was allergic to wheat. And then later to dairy, eggs, chicken, tree nuts and sesame. At one point, after a particularly bad reaction for which we couldn't pinpoint the cause, we even investigated an allergy to latex.

I was overwhelmed, confused, but also intrigued. What was going on? I spent the next few years reading research papers and books, stalking allergists (not literally, obviously) and attending seminars on food allergies and eczema. It became my mission to understand the two conditions. The more I researched them, the more interesting things got.

I wanted to understand allergies well enough to keep my child safe and also explain the condition easily and coherently enough to advocate for her (and others like her). In the process, I began helping other people understand eczema and allergies, writing articles and giving talks to parenting groups and schools. Every time I heard of a child dying from food allergies, it hit me hard but it strengthened my resolve to educate more people. These tragedies were unnecessary and often avoidable.

My family started off with severe allergies to six foods and heat-induced anaphylaxis. In the last seven years, we have seen close to 20 anaphylactic reactions, undergone several oral food challenges and years of oral immunotherapy to dairy, eggs and wheat. My baby has now outgrown those three allergies and for her seventh birthday we had our first-ever party with store-bought food! Although the journey has been harrowing at times, my children are thriving. Meanwhile, I've grown tremendously. What once stopped my life in its tracks is now my passion, my work, and my mission.

My hope is that this book, which has been years in the making, will help you on your allergy journey. It brings together explanations of scientific research and practical tips on living with wheat allergy. It is the manual I wish I had had while navigating the allergy minefield in the first few years.

In the words of Mary Ann Evans, the English novelist who went by the pen name 'George Eliot', "What do we live for, if it is not to make life less difficult to [sic] each other?"

HOW TO USE THIS BOOK

In this guide, we'll focus specifically on wheat allergy. Although it is one of the most common foods to cause serious allergic reactions, wheat allergy is not taken as seriously as peanut and nut allergies by the general public. The gluten-free health craze fuelled by social media doesn't help matters, with people thinking that minor bloating after a carb-heavy meal is the same as an allergy to wheat. It is not. This can make finding childcare options difficult and scary, as well as affecting virtually every aspect of a family's life.

Of my child's multiple food allergies, managing the wheat one was the most difficult. Wheat is everywhere, in many everyday foods, cosmetics and even toys. Whereas classrooms are often peanut and nut free, they are almost never free of any other allergen. This makes school, extracurricular classes and even social gatherings feel very dangerous.

This guide is based on the philosophy of less but better. Though not exhaustive, it is designed to be fairly comprehensive. It will help you gain a good enough understanding of allergies to ask your doctor the right questions and advocate for yourself in most situations (work, school, social, travel etc). You'll learn how to live *well* with allergies – without constant anxiety – while staying safe.

In my years helping families with food allergies and eczema, my motto has been 'Acceptance, Awareness, Action'. This book is split into three parts bearing the same names, albeit in a different order.

In Part 1, Awareness, we will explore what allergies are, and what they are not, as well as look at conditions like lactose intolerance and eosinophilic oesophagitis. We'll even look at some theories on what might be causing allergies.

Part 2, Acceptance, looks at the psychological side of living with allergies and will equip you with tools to lower your anxiety and bolster your resilience and confidence.

In Part 3, Action, we look at everything you need to live with allergies. We'll cover allergy tests, immunotherapy, reading labels, food substitutions, travelling and more.

Each section has short chapters on specific topics. You can read the book cover to cover or, if you have particular events coming up, like allergy tests or travel for example, you can start at the relevant chapter and then go back for context later.

There are also 'Helpful Hints' scattered through the book that give you step-by-step instructions on how to make certain situations smoother, like giving medication to a baby or introducing new foods. These are also listed in the contents page for easy reference as needed.

The symptoms of an allergic reaction are listed several times throughout the book. This is in an attempt to make them more familiar so that recognising a reaction becomes second nature.

Part 4 looks to the future. We will explore some promising research as well as possible discoveries and therapies on the horizon.

For more information on what exactly happens in the body during an allergic reaction, as well as a look at the key cells and antibodies involved, refer to the Further Reading section at the end of the book where it is all explained.

PART 1: AWARENESS
UNDERSTANDING ALLERGIES

Knowledge is the antidote to fear.
-- Ralph Waldo Emerson, essayist, poet and popular philosopher

Allergies can be scary, overwhelming and confusing. This section aims to empower you by arming you with knowledge. We will explore the difference between immediate and delayed reactions, as well as look into coeliac disease and gluten hypersensitivity.

Although there will be a focus on wheat allergy, you'll also learn about other common allergens and what you can do to prevent a child becoming allergic to those foods. We'll then delve into the million-dollar question – what causes allergies?

You will, hopefully, emerge less afraid and more confident at managing allergies in day-to-day life, explaining it to others and asking your doctor the right questions.

There are tools to deal with the fear, anxiety, isolation, and mental health in Part 2, while all the practicalities of managing allergies will be covered in Part 3.

Chapter 1
Allergies 101

In order to live with allergies, it helps to understand them so here it is in a nutshell (no pun intended).

An allergic reaction occurs when the immune system sees a certain protein as a threat and mounts an attack to protect the body. The protein is called the allergen and is usually harmless for most people.

There are two types of reactions - immediate and delayed.

Immediate reactions are driven by an antibody called immunoglobulin E (IgE) and are therefore also called *IgE-mediated allergies*. They are fast - taking between 30 seconds and 30 minutes to start - and occur every time the offending item is eaten or inhaled. A systemic reaction, involving more than one system in the body, is classified as *anaphylaxis*. A severe anaphylactic reaction can be fatal.

Delayed reactions can be seen between two and 72 hours after the food is eaten. They do not involve the same antibody and are called *non-IgE mediated allergies*. These reactions are not as well understood although they are still being researched. So far, we know that they involve a different part of the immune system acting on the digestive (gastrointestinal) system. Symptoms are seen along the digestive tract in the gullet, food pipe, stomach and small or large intestines and can continue for days or even weeks if the foods that trigger reactions continue to be consumed. Delayed reactions are covered in more detail in Chapter 2.

Children are more likely than adults to have food allergies with approximately 8% of kids affected by dairy allergy for example. However, the numbers come down with age as immune systems mature and allergies are outgrown.

Symptoms of an Allergic Reaction

An IgE-mediated allergic reaction will not necessarily look the same each time, even in the same person exposed to the same allergen. It is therefore important to be aware of the different signs that are possible. Symptoms tend to be seen in areas of the body where *mast cells* are concentrated, i.e. lining of the skin, nose, eyes, lungs, gut and blood vessels.

Someone having an immediate reaction might have the following symptoms that seem to have appeared out of the blue:

- Flushed face, hives, rash, itchy skin
- Swelling of eyes, face, throat, or tongue
- Persistent clearing of the throat, coughing, trouble breathing, speaking or swallowing
- Itchy, runny or blocked nose
- Abdominal cramps, diarrhoea, vomiting
- Faintness, paleness, or weakness as blood pressure drops. This can lead to loss of consciousness

The person may also experience anxiety or distress. This is often described as 'a sense of impending doom' as the person feels their body going into overdrive.

Anaphylaxis

A *systemic* allergic reaction, i.e. involving the whole body, is classified as anaphylaxis. According to Dr Philippe Bégin from the Université de Montréal, all IgE-mediated allergic reactions to food are systemic, with symptoms seen all around the body, and therefore anaphylactic. This is in contrast to *localised* reactions seen in conditions like 'pollen food oral allergy syndrome' or 'allergic rhinitis' (hay fever) where the symptoms are seen only where the allergen has touched the body, i.e. itching or swelling in the mouth, throat, nose, eyes etc.

Anaphylaxis can be life-threatening. It must be treated promptly and monitored in the hospital. There seem to be a few different views on what criteria indicate severe anaphylaxis requiring the use of epinephrine. Below are three that I have heard.

Severe anaphylaxis is when:
- either the respiratory or circulatory system is involved.
- symptoms are seen in the skin plus one other system, i.e. hives and any symptoms involving breathing, digestion or circulation.
- symptoms are seen in *any* two of the following systems: skin, breathing, digestion and circulation.

I think the last definition is the clearest, and the safest. My child has had hives and profuse vomiting within minutes of consuming a food. Without a doubt, this was a systemic reaction - anaphylaxis - that was progressing fast and must be treated immediately. Had we waited until she was having trouble breathing, as per the first definition, it might have been too late. I doubt any doctors would disagree.

For more on treating an allergic reaction, refer to Chapter 17.

:: Helpful Hint: How Much Causes a Reaction?

Allergic reactions vary between individuals. The amount of protein that causes a reaction, i.e. the *minimum tolerable dose*, for one person can be perfectly fine for another person with the same allergy.

For everyone, however, the size of an allergic reaction is *dose dependent*. This means that once they go past the minimum amount that causes a reaction for them, any increase will normally elicit a bigger reaction (think "more soap gives more bubbles").

If the body is exposed to the allergen under certain circumstances, a faster/larger than usual reaction can be seen. These 'co-factors' put the body under stress and stimulate certain cells that are central to allergic reactions.

Co-factors that lower the amount of the allergen that the body can tolerate include:

- Vigorous exercise
- Illness, e.g. a virus
- Menstrual period
- Mental stress or tiredness
- Sleep deprivation
- Exposure to other allergens e.g. during hay fever season
- Alcohol consumption
- Asthma or eczema flare-up

When intentionally exposing the body to a potential or known allergen, e.g. introducing a new food, oral food challenge, or oral immunotherapy, try to avoid the above situations if possible.

Chapter 2
Delayed Reactions: EoE, FPIES and FPIAP

Reactions to food that are seen hours or days after something is eaten fall under the umbrella of delayed or *non-IgE mediated food allergy*. The terms cover a range of gastrointestinal conditions that are not as well understood as the immediate (IgE-mediated) allergies described in the first chapter. Symptoms can be seen along the full length of the gut - throat to bottom - and can include:

- Abdominal discomfort or pain
- Vomiting
- Loose, frequent stools
- Constipation
- Colic
- Reflux
- Raw, red diaper rash
- Blood or mucous in stools
- Faltering growth in children

Diagnosing a delayed reaction to a food can be difficult as these same symptoms can sometimes be seen in a perfectly healthy non-allergic baby too. Or they may indicate an entirely different problem. The key, when trying to establish what is happening, is to log symptoms and watch for frequency (how often) and duration (how many days in a row).

Determining and managing delayed food allergies requires the involvement of a specialist called a gastroenterologist. There are no laboratory tests to confirm non-IgE mediated allergies. The most effective test is the *eliminate-rechallenge process*, where the suspected trigger, e.g. wheat, is removed for a period of at least two weeks and then reintroduced gradually to see if symptoms reappear. This process must be done under the guidance of a doctor or dietician.

Eosinophilic Oesophagitis (EoE) affects the gullet in the throat or oesophagus (food pipe). It occurs when special white blood cells, called *eosinophils*, deposit in the lining of the oesophagus. The resulting inflammation can cause difficulty swallowing, vomiting and a failure to gain weight in babies. The doctor will examine the oesophagus and perform a biopsy as part of the diagnosis process.

Common allergens that trigger EoE include milk, egg, and wheat, although other foods like soy, nuts and seafood can also play a part. The condition is often seen in people with seasonal pollen allergies or asthma, and the number of people affected by it seems to be rising. Babies with EoE may outgrow it in the first few years of life. When EoE arises in older children and adults, symptoms tend not to resolve.

Food Protein Induced Enterocolitis Syndrome (FPIES) affects the small and large intestine. It causes severe vomiting, and sometimes diarrhoea, in infants soon after the first introduction of certain foods. Symptoms are typically seen two to four hours after the food is eaten. Children can become pale and floppy during a reaction. Milk and soy are the most common offenders, although other foods like grains, particularly rice, or meats can also cause a reaction. FPIES is not very common and can be misdiagnosed initially. The condition often resolves by preschool age.

Food Protein Induced Allergic Proctocolitis (FPIAP) affects the large intestine and presents with blood, and sometimes mucous, in the stool of very young infants. The babies are otherwise healthy and growing well. Symptoms start at 1-4 weeks of age. Although it is often seen in breastfed infants, it can occur in formula-fed babies as well. The main causes for the condition are cow's milk and soy. To confirm the diagnosis in breastfeeding babies, the mother will have to complete the eliminate-rechallenge process too. FPIAP resolves in 50% of babies by six months of age and in 95% of children by nine months.

It is possible to have both IgE-mediated and non-IgE mediated food allergies.

Chapter 3
Ghastly Gluten

With all the publicity around peanut allergy most people may think that the legume-of-choice of circus elephants everywhere is the only thing that causes serious allergic reactions. As we know, this is not true. In fact, wheat is one of the top allergens in the world. It is part of a list of foods called the 'priority allergens' which are responsible for more than 90% of allergic reactions. We'll cover more on this in Chapter 5.

Wheat allergy, like most food allergies, is more common in kids than adults. Although numbers have not been clearly established, it is thought to affect between 0.5% to 3% of children. However, research has shown that nearly a third (29%) of these children outgrow it by age four and nearly two-thirds (65%) by age 12.

There are four different types of proteins in wheat - gliadin, glutenin, globulin and albumin. What we commonly refer to as 'gluten' is actually made up of two smaller proteins called gliadin and glutenin, which represent roughly 80% of the protein in wheat flour. They bind together when water is mixed with wheat flour, forming long, elastic loops of gluten.

Gluten gets its name from the Latin word for 'gluey' (*conglutinosus*). It forms a binding matrix in dough which helps bread to rise by trapping carbon dioxide, and gives wheat products like bread and pasta their chewy, satisfying texture. As the amount of wheat in the typical Western diet has increased, so have techniques to cultivate a crop that yields lighter, more tasty bread - with more gluten. It is therefore not surprising that the incidence of adverse reactions to wheat has also increased.

Coeliac Disease

Coeliac disease is an autoimmune condition where the immune system attacks the lining of the gut, particularly the intestines, if the person consumes foods containing gluten. The resulting inflammation causes symptoms like diarrhoea, bloating, abdominal cramps, nausea, tiredness and in some cases a rash called 'dermatitis herpetiformis'. The damage to the gut makes it difficult to absorb the nutrients in food, sometimes causing poor growth or delayed puberty in children and weight loss in adults.

The condition is diagnosed through a blood test called a 'coeliac screen', while the person still has gluten in the diet. A gut biopsy will also be done for confirmation and to assess the extent of the damage to the gut.

The three cereals containing gluten are wheat, rye and barley. Once these are removed from the diet, symptoms should subside, allowing the body to heal. Some people may also be sensitive to oats as they are normally cross-contaminated with wheat. This is because farmers often alternate the two crops to maintain soil health. However, with the rise in demand, it is becoming easier to find gluten-free oats that are grown on dedicated lots.

Coeliac (sometimes spelled celiac) disease is not an allergy or an intolerance. It is an autoimmune condition. Although both allergies and autoimmune diseases involve an overreaction of the immune system, the conditions are very different in nature. In an autoimmune disease, the body is effectively attacking itself, not a foreign protein, and tissues are destroyed. An allergic response is the body's attempt to expel the unwanted invader. A distinct set of genes tend to dominate whether autoimmune diseases develop which makes it easier to determine who will have them. With allergies, it is not as clear cut.

Gluten Hypersensitivity

A food intolerance describes when the body cannot digest the sugars in a food. It is very different from an allergy. Although the symptoms can be very uncomfortable, there is no lasting damage (as in the case of conditions like eosinophilic oesophagitis) and it is not potentially fatal (like IgE-mediated allergy).

Enzymes are chemicals that break down the sugars in foods for the body to use. There is a specific enzyme for each sugar. The name of the sugar usually ends in '-ose' and its corresponding enzyme ends in '-ase'. An intolerance occurs when the body produces too little or none of the enzyme needed for digestion. For example, in the case of dairy, there is not enough lactase (enzyme) produced in the small intestine to break down lactose (sugar). Once the undigested lactose moves into the large intestine, it ferments. The resulting acids and gases cause bloating, cramps and flatulence.

Gluten is a protein not a sugar and although the term 'gluten intolerance' seems to be rife in the world of social media, it is not recognised as a condition by the medical community. Some people do seem to be sensitive to gluten, experiencing bloating, cramps and/or headaches when they eat certain cereals. Although symptoms seem to clear when gluten is avoided, they have a negative coeliac screen and no evidence of damage to the gut on biopsy. This condition is termed 'non-coeliac gluten hypersensitivity' and is not well understood.

Managing a food sensitivity can be a bit of an art according to paediatric gastroenterologist Dr Cynthia Popalis. There is usually a threshold below which a gluten sensitive person can tolerate the protein without symptoms. This may be some breadcrumbs on a fish finger, a dash of soy sauce in a stir-fry or something else altogether. Finding a happy medium requires some willingness on the part of the patient to experiment and the knowledge that symptoms will pass.

Chapter 4
Mistaken Identities: Is It Really Allergy?

In the last seven years, I have found myself in a lot of conversations about allergies. Most people I meet claim to either have food allergies themselves or have a family member who does. If they were correct, this would point to at least half the population having food allergies! Common logic tells us this cannot be true.

In fact, studies have repeatedly shown that only a small proportion of people who think they have allergies are correct. In 2008, parents of nearly 1000 children were asked if their children had food allergies. Approximately 35% reported that they did but when the children were tested, only 5% were actually diagnosed with allergies.

There are four main reasons so many people may think they have food allergies when in fact they do not.

1. Confusing food intolerance and allergy (e.g. lactose intolerance vs milk allergy).
2. Food poisoning
3. Self-diagnosis
4. Misinformation from alternative healthcare practitioners

Let's look at each of these in a little more detail.

Hard to Tolerate

As explained in the previous chapter, food intolerance or sensitivity is very different from food allergy. Intolerance involves the digestive system and not the immune system, and food sugars not food proteins. Although the symptoms can be very uncomfortable they are not potentially fatal as in the case of allergy and there is no lasting damage like in coeliac disease.

Upset-Me-Not

The body, every body, has defences against certain things. We sneeze when we sniff ground pepper, cough in a smoky room, and have upset stomachs if we eat spoiled foods. Food poisoning occurs when the immune system mounts an all-out war against harmful bacteria in food. Symptoms include vomiting, diarrhoea, cramps, dizziness and weakness. Although this does involve the immune system (albeit a different part), the reaction is against an actual dangerous microorganism, not a benign food protein. Symptoms would be seen in anyone and everyone.

Paging Dr Google

There are 100 million internet searches related to allergies every year. Parenting forums are chock-full of posts about allergies especially from parents worried about fussiness, bloating, constipation etc. But these symptoms may have nothing to do with allergies. Although diet is often blamed for colic - unexplained, prolonged crying in the evenings - research has shown that is very unlikely. Colic is now thought to be related to the baby's nervous system adapting to the sudden increase in stimulation, including lights and sounds, after nine months in the quiet, dark womb.

We've all consulted the internet at some point for health questions and it is undoubtedly a great resource, but the part the internet, and in fact this book, should play in your health is to help you formulate a list of good questions for your doctor, not to replace her.

Beware of Snake Oil

It is tempting, when dealing with unwanted symptoms with no known cause, to grasp at any solutions being offered. And if you are looking for confirmation of 'allergies' then it's not hard to find.

Tests galore in cities all over the world as well as the internet offering a one-stop answer to lethargy, hyperactivity, bloating or skin issues.

Even some independent health-food shops offer to identify lists of allergens using tests that have no scientific basis. Some of these tests are actually quite creative if you stop to think about it but almost none (apart from the ones covered in the Chapter 14) are proven to be accurate.

In fact, although interpreting intolerance or food poisoning as allergies could be deemed an honest mistake, the wrong information from these tests are deliberately misleading and can be downright dangerous. In addition to being a waste of money, they tend to produce long lists of 'allergens' which in turn promote unnecessary 'treatments' and restrictive diets that can cause real harm. I once met a young lady who proudly told me she had a list of 82 'allergens'. Needless to say, she was not the picture of health.

Some commonly-found bogus tests are described in Chapter 13.

Accurate diagnosis of any health condition is vital. The wrong diagnosis can often mean unnecessary medications and/or dietary exclusions - both leading to serious health problems. For example, proton pump inhibitors which are sometimes used to treat reflux can impair iron absorption. Using iron supplements to treat this can then cause constipation, which may also need treatment thereby continuing the cycle.

More worrying however, can be the effects from restricting diets without the proper medical guidance. In 2017, news of an 11-year old Canadian boy who went blind from a restrictive diet made headlines. In an attempt to curb his eczema, the boy's parents limited his diet to just lamb, pork, apples, cucumbers, potatoes and Cheerios. Although their motive, like most parents', was well-meaning, much of the damage to his vision was permanent.

Chapter 5
The VIP List: Priority Allergens

It is theoretically possible to be allergic to any protein but certain foods are responsible for over 90% of food allergies. These are called 'priority allergens' and are the ones to watch out for when introducing solids to your infant. This is especially true if your child already has eczema or asthma as these conditions make him/her more likely to develop food allergies.

In the US, the priority allergens are

- Dairy
- Eggs
- Fish
- Shellfish including crustaceans and molluscs (e.g. shrimp, crab, lobster, clams etc)
- Peanut (which as a legume, not a nut, is closer to lentils or soy than almonds)
- Tree nuts (e.g. almonds, pistachios, cashews etc)
- Soybean
- Wheat
- Sesame

In Canada, the list also includes

- Mustard
- Sulphites/sulphur dioxide

And in the UK and European Union, the major allergen list contains all of the above as well as

- All cereals containing gluten, including wheat

- Lupin
- Celery

The top allergens down under in Australia and New Zealand are all of the above except mustard, sulphites and celery.

Being identified on the list of priority allergens by a country's authorities means that by law the food item must be declared clearly in the ingredients list of any packaged food being sold. In the US, sesame has only recently been added to the priority allergen list and does not legally need to be highlighted as an ingredient until 2023.

When travelling to a country where your allergen is not on the priority list, you will need to be more thorough when reading labels. For more on reading labels, see Chapter 18. If you are considering travelling with allergies, refer to Chapter 21.

Chapter 6
Balloons, Bees and Barbells: Non-Food Allergens

If you thought severe allergic reactions could only be caused by foods, think again. Anaphylaxis can have the following non-food causes too.

Insect Stings

The main offenders for causing anaphylaxis are in the flying flower-friendly category, i.e. honeybees, wasps, hornets and yellow jackets, but fire ants are also known to cause allergic reactions in around 1% of people.

With the rise in demand for 'natural' products, people who are allergic to bee stings need to be careful of bee products like royal jelly (the food made by the queen bee for her workers) and bee propolis (the glue bees use to seal gaps in the beehive).

Latex

Balloons, rubber dishwashing gloves, tennis balls, condoms, exercise bands... Latex is everywhere. And for people who are allergic to natural rubber latex, that makes the world a little bit more dangerous. Around half of people allergic to latex also react to fruits like banana, avocado, chestnut, kiwi, passion fruit, papaya, plum, strawberry and/or tomato as the proteins in these foods have a similar structure to latex.

Medications

Some drugs like antibiotics from the penicillin family, muscle relaxants given during general anaesthesia and painkillers (e.g. aspirin and ibuprofen) can cause allergic reactions in some individuals. According to the American College of Allergy, Asthma and Immunology there is no familial link so if a parent is allergic it does not mean their children also need to avoid these medications unless they too experience a reaction. It is important not to confuse side effects, that anyone might experience, with allergy which is quite rare as this limits the medications available for use.

In addition, penicillin allergy is rarely lifelong and 80% of people lose the allergy once they have avoided the drug for 10 years. This highlights the need to review allergies and tests with a board-certified allergist regularly to keep diagnoses up-to-date.

Exercise

If ever there was a good excuse not to work out, this would be it, but exercise-induced anaphylaxis is rare. It is sometimes, though not always, related to a protein in wheat called omega-5-gliadin.

Unknown

Sometimes the cause of an anaphylactic reaction is not food or any of the above and is simply not known. Despite the doctors' best efforts to investigate the cause, it remains a mystery.

Chapter 7
What Causes Allergies?

There is a great deal of research going into allergies and some theories on how food allergies start are now well-established. These involve:

- our genes
- the balance of microorganisms in our bodies
- the route by which our bodies are first exposed to foods
- the timing of introduction to foods
- vitamin D

Nice Genes!

Allergies have a genetic component but they are not necessarily hereditary. This means that although there are genes being switched on or off (genetic), having an allergic parent does not always mean children with the same, if any, allergies.

Having said that, *atopy* runs in families and makes one more allergy-prone. Atopy is the genetic tendency to develop immune responses involving the antibody immunoglobulin E (IgE) to common proteins in the environment like pollens or foods. Typical atopic diseases are allergic rhinitis (hay fever), asthma and eczema. Together, these are called the 'atopic triad'. Having one parent with an atopic disease, particularly atopic eczema, makes a child likely to develop one too. The odds increase if both parents have an atopic disease, or if either parent has more than one, e.g. eczema and hay fever.

The 'allergic march' refers to the progression from one atopic disease to the next. Having one condition makes a person more likely to develop another. It usually starts with atopic eczema in the first few months of life. The child may then go on to develop food allergies and/or asthma, typically at around 12-18 months, and seasonal hay fever after age two. As IgE is involved in all of the conditions, this is sometimes also called the 'atopic march'.

Interestingly, the way to stop the march progressing may be literally at our fingertips. Multiple studies have shown that babies with severe eczema are more likely to go on to become allergic to food and/or asthmatic in later childhood. Treating eczema promptly and aggressively could therefore be the key to preventing life-long suffering from food allergies and asthma.

Switched On

The number of people with allergies is rising rapidly. Although better diagnosis is likely to have an effect on the statistics, some allergies are increasing too fast to be attributed to just better testing methods or even human genes changing over time. According to Prof George Du Toit from King's College London, peanut allergy seems to be doubling every 20 years, pointing to an *epigenetic* component. The prefix *epi* means 'above' so an epigenetic factor is something above genes, in our outside environment, switching them on and off.

The role of bacteria, in particular the gut and skin microbiomes, has been extensively studied. A gut filled with health-promoting bacteria, fungi and yeast forms the foundation of wellbeing. The Hygiene Hypothesis, further developed to become the Old Friends Mechanism, claims that we are being too clean. This also has some merit. The overuse of antibiotics and antibacterial disinfectants reduces our exposure to the microbes that prevent our immune system from overreacting. However, the theory that having more childhood infections - like colds and chickenpox - can reduce allergies, has been discounted.

The role of the microbiome may partly explain why allergies are seen more in babies born by caesarean section as they do not receive the transfer of microorganisms from the mother that would be seen in a vaginal birth. Babies who are breastfed also receive beneficial bacteria from the mother's skin on top of the nutrients and antibodies in the milk itself.

Getting a HEAD Start

While we are removing microorganisms from our environment, we are adding food stuff to the things we touch on a daily basis. The drive towards 'natural' products means that there are foods in our skin creams, soaps, shampoos, and makeup. This is a big problem, especially where there is eczema involved, as one ground-breaking theory showed.

Studies have shown that many children, particularly those with eczema, who used skin products containing peanuts or wheat went on to develop allergies to these foods. It was also found that babies in households where peanuts were eaten were more likely to become allergic, but that if the infants were also fed peanuts regularly before the age of one, they did not develop the allergy.

Research by Prof Gideon Lack at King's College London looked at whether allergies might be caused when the immune system encounters foods for the first time through the skin and not the mouth. He called this the Dual-Allergen Exposure Hypothesis. Using the analogy of the body being a house, he likened it to the protein sneaking in through a window instead of entering through the front door. This is especially true in babies with eczema, where the damaged skin could be seen as a broken window providing easy access to the house.

Personally, this blew my mind. I ate egg and cheese sandwiches on sesame-encrusted wheat bread every day while breastfeeding my newborn baby who had severe, exposed eczema. My child developed wheat, dairy, egg and sesame allergy (among others). However, I wasn't the only one bowled over by this idea. Researchers have repeatedly tested this hypothesis and multiple scientific studies have shown that the theory holds.

Many other studies have also shown that the earlier eczema develops and the more severe it is, the more likely it is that food allergies will develop. Extensive, exposed eczema that begins early in life is the biggest risk factor for food allergies. Despite what many people think, allergies don't cause eczema, eczema causes allergies!

Taking a LEAP Forward

Up until very recently, parents were routinely told that they should not under any circumstances give highly allergenic foods to babies until a certain age. Absolutely not. No way Jose. None. Nada. Niente. For example, to eat eggs little Johnny would have to wait until he turned one, and to have some of his sister's peanut butter sandwich he'd have to wait until his third birthday.

Then in January 2017, health authorities around the world did the kind of 180-degree flip usually seen in kung-fu movies, saying that not only *can* you introduce risky foods like peanuts to your 6-month old, but that you *should*.

The advice is based on a study published in early 2015 called LEAP (Learning Early About Peanut). Researchers in London (again at King's College and led by Prof Du Toit and Prof Lack) noticed that ten times as many children in the UK were peanut allergic compared to in Israel. The numbers were hugely divergent even when looking at just Jewish children in the UK, i.e. with similar genetic profiles. The doctors suspected that diet could be playing a role. Not only are Israeli parents not told to avoid peanuts, they routinely give it to babies. In fact, Bamba, a very common teething snack in Israel, is made with peanuts.

The researchers then took two groups of Jewish British families with babies ages between four and 11 months. One group stuck to the conventional guidelines of avoiding peanuts, while the other group introduced it into the babies' diets and kept it in regularly. Of the children in the study who did consume peanuts regularly, only 3% developed an allergy by the time they turned 5, compared to 17% in the group who avoided the legume completely. That's nearly six times as many children who became allergic from avoiding peanuts.

My daughter's first anaphylactic reaction (to wheat) happened to coincide with the publication of the LEAP study and, once our paediatric allergist explained the findings of the study to us, we agreed to be her first case. Our child was one of the first patients in Canada to try out the new advice and it worked.

A subsequent study, called EAT, by the same group of researchers showed that using early introduction to prevent allergy also holds true for eggs. Adding egg into a child's diet very early on does prevent egg allergy. However, it was not as clear cut with the other foods - dairy, wheat, fish and sesame. This may be because the body reacts to these proteins differently or, more likely, due to poorer compliance. Families found it more difficult to stick to the regime of all six foods in the EAT trial as compared to just peanuts in the LEAP trial. Also, the fact that babies under six months have tiny tummies that can't hold much food probably played a part!

Hello Sunshine!

Vitamin D seems to have an effect on allergy development. One study revealed that there are more EpiPen prescriptions in northern US states that are further from the equator and get less sunshine, than in southern states. Other studies indicated that although vitamin D does seem to play a part in avoiding allergies, it is not as clear cut as achieving a target level of vitamin D in the blood.

What we can see is that there are many pieces to the puzzle of why allergies develop. These include genes, the gut and skin microbiomes, presence of eczema and its severity, the timing and route of food introduction and vitamin D levels. There are many other factors that are still being researched, some of which are discussed in Part 4.

:: Helpful Hint: Lowering the Risk of Allergies

Below are a few actions that, according to scientific findings, *may* help stop allergies developing.

- <u>Don't eliminate foods unnecessarily</u>: Randomised controlled trials showed there was no benefit, in terms of allergy development, in pregnant women restricting their diets. Eat well so that your baby grows well and is exposed to many tastes and smells.

- <u>Safety first</u>: Although there are many benefits to a natural vaginal birth, including the microbiome transfer, the best option of all is one where both mum and baby are safe. If a caesarean-section is medically necessary, do it.

- <u>Don't be anti-antibiotics</u>: Some bacteria are health-promoting, others are dangerous. Babies are very vulnerable and antibiotics can save lives. If antibiotics are clinically necessary to help your baby, don't refuse them.

- <u>Breast is ideal but not best</u>: Breastfeed if you can and for as long as you can. If breastfeeding isn't in the cards, don't beat yourself up. The best milk for your baby is the one they can get regularly so that they can grow and thrive.

- <u>Introduce early, introduce often</u>: Introduce foods between four to 11 months of age, focusing those on the priority allergen list in Chapter 6.

- <u>Treat eczema</u>: Get atopic dermatitis under control and halt the atopic march.

- Avoid antibacterial disinfectants: Clean with soap and water. If it's strong enough to kill the dreaded Coronavirus, it's good enough to clean your family and your home.

- Aim for equanimity: Realise you can do everything 'right' and still develop allergies. As with most things in life, there are no guarantees.

PART 2: ACCEPTANCE
BUILDING MENTAL STRENGTH

Happiness can exist only in acceptance
-- George Orwell, novelist, author and critic

To say that living with allergies can be difficult is an understatement. Over and above the stress of reading, then rereading labels, sourcing the right products, doctors' appointments full of jargon and the social isolation, it is the constant anxiety of having another reaction that is the hardest. The fact that allergic reactions can be fatal is the cherry on top.

A person with food allergies may grow out of them. But they may not. No amount of hand wringing or self-pity will change anything. There's no way around it. The only way out is through.

This section of the book addresses the mental struggle of living with food allergies. Although it is significant, the psychological side of food allergies is an often-overlooked aspect. Just as mental health is at the centre of your battle with food allergies, so it is at the centre of this book. It is not an afterthought.

I have read anonymous posts online of desperate families taking a holiday without the allergic child in order to have a break, or even mothers wanting to give children up. Although I was slightly horrified, I was also wholly empathetic. My mental health has suffered immensely at times during this journey. My hope is that using the advice in this section, you will not reach such a desperate state.

Most food allergy deaths occur in the tween to early-20s age group, where peer pressure and a desire to fit in can drive young people to engage in risky behaviour. At a seminar on food allergies, the doctors spoke of a teenager hiding in the bathroom while having an allergic reaction as he was too embarrassed to seek help. Luckily, he was fine. There have been others who were not as fortunate.

My hope is that if we build confidence and resilience in our children, this will act as an inoculation against unnecessary risk-taking, thereby saving some lives. And in any case, who doesn't want confident, assertive, resilient kids?

The following chapters will give you mental tools to get through the initial period of adjusting to life with food allergies and beyond. The self-care and mental-health skills you will develop should help you live as full and normal a life as possible. We will look at the importance of support, tools to build resilience and confidence and even touch on sleep and meditation.

Chapter 8
Focus on Feelings

Dealing with food allergies, especially at the beginning, can bring about a rollercoaster of emotions and feelings. Although there can be the relief from finally having a diagnosis and treatment plan, there is the fear of another reaction, the stress of doctor's appointments and tests, and perhaps the dread of social situations. You might even find yourself needing to feel an absolute sense of control in every aspect of your life, as I did. This, in reality, is just not possible.

Interestingly, those who have had allergic reactions tend to have a better quality of life than those who have been labelled allergic but never had a reaction, according to Dr Philippe Bégin from Université de Montréal. This actually makes sense. Although reactions can be terrifying and traumatic, once you have experienced one (or several), you know what to expect. Identifying symptoms and getting treatment become easier and faster.

Anxiety

Feeling anxious is part and parcel of this journey, especially for an allergy parent. Once you accept this, you can do something about it.

Parental anxiety is highly correlated to children's anxiety. Kids mirror what they see from the people they trust most - mum and dad. This fact stunned me during my baby's first anaphylactic reaction. While the doctors at our holiday resort fumbled around trying to assess our baby, she kept her eyes firmly on me. She was relatively calm because (outwardly) I seemed calm. In other situations, I have panicked and/or lost my cool, and so have all my kids (the two I gave birth to and the one I married).

Model Behaviour

The next time you are feeling overwhelmed, anxious or stressed, instead of gritting your teeth and pushing any emotions under the carpet, talk about it. Does the feeling give you sweaty palms? Butterflies in your stomach? A pounding heart? If you have children, this will also help them by giving them the tools to recognise their feelings and the vocabulary to voice them.

Naming feelings and their physical symptoms takes away their power over us. You'll start to be able to take a step back and notice "this is anxiety" and then once the physical symptoms have passed, you'll notice that you are no longer feeling anxious. It will pass. This knowledge that everything is transient and nothing is permanent will help develop a more positive mindset.

Recognise that it is normal to experience the full rainbow of emotions and that there are actions you can take to ease any distress. Help your children understand this too by modelling what to do. Verbalise the feeling and the action. Below are some examples.

"I'm feeling tired so I'm going to lie down and listen to some soothing music."
"I'm feeling a bit sad so I'm going to call a friend."
"I'm feeling anxious so I'm going for a walk."

Talk, Talk

Take time to talk and listen as a family. Every day, you could each say what went well that day, what was tricky (not "bad"), and one thing that made you feel grateful. This could be done at a mealtime, at bedtime or anytime you choose, as long as you are consistent. This great ritual helps the family bond, gives everyone a voice and fosters a positive mindset. Talking openly about experiences, positive and difficult, can help develop resilience in children in the same way that journaling helps adults.

When someone brings up something they are worried about, don't just soothe them, coach them.
- Challenge negative statements ("Do you *never* get to eat *any* of the food at the birthday party or just sometimes?") and help find examples from the past to disprove their worries.
- Help the person come up with solutions by asking the right questions. For example, "What could we do to make the birthday party safer for you?". By making a list together and voicing concerns, you can both come away empowered for this situation and all similar ones in the future.

Allergy Play

Play is how children learn and it is how they process emotions and difficult experiences. If your child has allergies, or has seen someone having a reaction, you may notice it featuring in their play. Teddy may need a blood test or an injection in his thigh. Dolly might need to ask if there will be soy milk at the tea party. This is perfectly normal and really quite cute if you think about it.

:: Helpful Hint: Stop the Spiral in 1, 2, 3, 4, 5

If you are feeling overwhelmed and things are starting to spiral downwards, here are a few techniques to help. They are all rooted in sound science. You can pick any that you like or work your way through all of them. Like a meditation habit, choosing to do these on a regular basis, not just in an emergency, can help you avoid the spirals in the first place.

1. <u>Body scan</u>: Sit or lie down, close your eyes and do a body scan for **one** minute. Start at the top of the head and work systematically down to see which muscles are clenched (e.g. forehead, jaw, shoulders, hands) and see if you can release them.

2. <u>Double breath</u>: Take **two** breaths in and then breathe out fully. This is called the *physiological sigh*, and involves taking a normal breath in through the nose, followed by a longer deeper breath in to expand the lungs further, then breathing out slowly through the mouth.

3. <u>Mindfulness trio</u>: Name **three** things that you can see, three things you can hear, and then three things you can feel.

4. <u>Square breathing</u>: Take a deep breath - counting to **four** - into your belly, feeling it expand like a balloon. Hold for four counts. Breathe out for four counts and hold again for four counts. Complete four breaths.

5. <u>Stretching</u>: Set a timer for **five** minutes, perhaps on your phone, and do any stretches or yoga postures that come to mind. This may end up being just one asana or a full sequence. It doesn't matter. Just keep going until the timer ends.

Chapter 9
What's the Story?

Your *self-story* is important, both as a person with allergies and as a caregiver. The story you tell yourself forms your identity and affects the way you approach any, and every, situation. Are you or your child an allergic person or a person who happens to have allergies? It matters.

Control the narrative

Ada had severe eczema as a baby. In fact, she was initially diagnosed with it at just 10-days old. Uncomfortable and itchy, she slept terribly, if at all. Then came the allergies. Oh so many allergies. Her first ever beach vacation also had her first ever ambulance ride. Her family stopped going on holidays. And to parties. Playdates were limited. Daycare was out of the question and, when the time came, a suitable school was very difficult to find.

Here's another way to look at the same story:

Ada got to spend the entirety of the first four years of her life in the company of the two people who loved her the most - her parents. They played, laughed, and ate the best foods for her diet. Because she had food allergies and eczema, she was monitored closely by some phenomenal doctors. Her playmates also happened to be scientists with four master's degrees between them and a fascination for child development and learning. This meant Ada was speaking in full sentences at 18 months, while also running, jumping and kicking a ball well ahead of her peers. She attended excellent schools with an emphasis on the whole child and she flourished in maths, science and English. She came up with her first invention at age three and started a charity at seven.

We in the allergy community are not victims, but warriors and heroes who triumph over adversity on a regular, if not daily, basis. Among other things, my daughter's allergies have helped her develop

- Courage and strength
- Resilience
- Eloquence and an enhanced ability to communicate
- Empathy
- Self-awareness
- Interest in and knowledge of science and medicine

Upon reflection, they've helped me develop the same skills too.

Resilience Resumé

Psychologists have identified four core beliefs central to building resilience in children:

1. They have some control over their lives.
2. They can learn from failure.
3. They matter as human beings.
4. They have real strengths to rely on and share.

We can use allergic reactions to build a 'resilience resumé' by using two more R words - reframing and retrospection.

Reframing is the act of looking at something with a slightly different perspective. To get away from the victim mentality, we can ask ourselves the following questions:

- What do I have control over?
- What is good about this situation?

Retrospection involves looking back at past experiences with an analytical mind to gain insights. For example:

- How much have we grown individually and as a family?
- What positives have come out of this?

Anchors and Assets

When it feels as though our world is spinning out of control, using our *anchors* and *assets* can help.

Anchors are things that stay the same, for example our routines, school/work, or favourite books. We all benefit from structure and predictability, not just children. Focus on what you can control. For me, decluttering our home, and our schedules, in the last few years has been an enormous help. When things start to feel chaotic, a review of my family's possessions and our time commitments gives me a sense of control. Starting down the path to minimalism has really helped ease the feeling of having too many spinning plates. It may help you too.

Our assets are our support network, i.e. "who is there for us?". The list could include parents, grandparents, siblings, friends, teachers, doctors, and colleagues. Mapping this out, literally, helps us feel more confident and able to cope.

Resilience is built among individuals too. This *collective resilience* comes from shared experiences, shared narratives and shared power. Finding and connecting with other food allergy families can be enormously helpful. Although the diagnosis of a health condition can elicit sympathy from many people (i.e. "I feel bad for you"), other people with similar experiences can provide *empathy* (i.e. "I actually understand"). Support groups, if you can find a suitable one, can provide this, as can food-allergy friends. The rise in food allergies means both of these are easier to find.

:: Helpful Hint: Self-Care

Self-care is not selfish. In fact, it is selfish not to take care of yourself as there are people counting on you to be healthy and sane. Here are some ideas on how to keep your reserves topped up:

- Meditation: There are many forms of meditation - mantra, mindfulness, transcendental etc. Find one that resonates with you, or if you're a newbie, start with the techniques in 'Helpful   Hints: Stop   the   Spiral'.

- Sleep: The jury is in. There are no awards for winning the sleep-deprivation competition. Sleep is critical for both physical   and   mental   well-being.

- Food: Work to keep your blood sugars stable. 'Hangry' is not   a   good   look   on   anyone.

- Fun: Make it a point to figure out what gives you and/or your child joy and incorporate this regularly into your life. In addition, plan special things - *superchargers* if you will - that you can anticipate.

- Humour: Maintain a sense of humour. Life with allergies can get very serious. Laughing can break even the most tense situation. Find ways to laugh whenever you can, whether by horsing around with your family, watching comedy on tv, or even classes like laughter yoga.

Find ways to process your emotions. Sports, music, art, journaling etc are all great outlets. Don't let allergies stop you from living a full life.

Chapter 10
A Note on 'Healthy' Food

Keto, slow-carb, low-carb, plant-based - 'healthy' eating has become a competitive sport.

Years ago, I went grocery shopping with a friend. We split up and grabbed a few things. When we met back up, she looked at the flaxseeds, chia seeds, and dried fruit in my cart - all healthy foods by most measures - and said to me, "Oh, don't you eat organic?". It still makes me laugh to this day.

Healthy food, by definition, is food that promotes good health. This is highly individualised. What is good for one person is not necessarily good for another. For example, while a banana is a powerhouse of micro and macro nutrients, it is effectively poison for a diabetic. In the case of food allergies, this is even more acute. A handful of nuts, a whey-protein packed green smoothie, a slice of artisan whole-grain wheat bread - all of these can be fatal within minutes for someone with the relevant allergies. To be healthy, you must first be alive.

There was a period when our first child was very young that we were completely and utterly overwhelmed. On top of six allergens and a suspected allergy to latex, we were battling with severe eczema, chronic bowel issues, and sleep that was so bad we were referred to a paediatric neurologist. We relied on biscuits and fries. Store bought biscuits full of sugar (although they were gluten free and organic!) and often McDonald's fries (minus the salt of course).

As much as we would have wanted to feed our baby organic free-range boiled eggs with beautifully cut soldiers of whole-grain seeded bread, or homemade chicken noodle soup, these were the opposite of healthy for her. In fact, McDonald's fries - which are cooked separately from anything else so have no exposure to any of the priority allergens - were infinitely better for her health than homemade chicken noodle soup with several of her allergens.

Of course, I am not by any means advocating a diet of fries and biscuits. I'm illustrating a point. In fact, the motive behind writing this book is to save overwhelmed, confused and stressed parents going through what we did. When you are in the eye of the storm, you just cannot think straight. The priority then is to survive, to grow, to work with your medical team. You can fix everything else later. Do what you need to survive and hopefully the tips in this book will help.

We knew, through the condescending looks and thinly-veiled snide comments from both strangers and friends, that people judged us. They still do. The thing is, there is plenty of evidence to show that restricted diets can lead to physical health problems and even eating disorders. Not only have my children always exceeded all their growth targets in height and weight, they are also incredibly secure, eloquent, happy and, most importantly, alive.

They eat well-balanced, albeit still somewhat restricted and picky, diets and genuinely enjoy fruit and vegetables. They don't crave sweets. We don't even have a bag of sugar in our house. That, my friends, is 'healthy'.

PART 3: ACTION
LIVING WITH ALLERGIES

You can't stop the waves, but you can learn to surf
-- Joseph Goldstein, meditation teacher

A few years ago, I attended an allergy awareness fundraising event. Towards the end, one of the organisers gave a speech in which he lamented that his allergic children would never enjoy the same carefree youth, filled with concerts and sporting events, as their parents. This baffled me. Why not? Sure, they would have to plan a few extra steps but there is nothing allergy children (and adults) cannot do.

This section is about living with allergies. The goal is to thrive, not merely survive. We will look at allergy tests and who should be administering them (spoiler alert - board-certified allergists only!) as well as what questions to ask your doctor as you formulate a plan together. We will discuss feeding babies, immunotherapy, medications, food substitutions and many things in between.

Living *well* with allergies is not easy, but it is not impossible. Instead of being paralysed with fear, our approach to allergies should be like our approach to cars. The thought of motor accidents can be terrifying but we don't keep ourselves or our kids from going near any roads or riding in vehicles. We emphasise road safety, teach everyone how and where to cross the street, and realise that we must use seat belts.

So buckle up, and let's get going.

Chapter 11
Kids with Food Allergies

A baby's first year can be particularly stressful and confusing for parents. Most food allergies tend to show up in early childhood and, according to paediatric allergist Dr Helen Brough, we hardly ever see a child with just one food allergy. Below is some guidance on some common questions related to allergies.

Breastfeeding

Although trace amounts of food proteins do pass into breastmilk, they are exactly that - trace amounts. For example, a study of breastmilk composition found that less than one millionth of the protein from cow's milk travels through to breast milk, too small an amount to trigger a reaction in most allergic children. As Dr Robert Boyle, one of the authors of the paper, put it, you would need roughly 1500 litres of breastmilk to get approximately 1mg of cow's milk protein.

Contrary to what the blogosphere and social media would have you believe, you do not have to avoid allergens while breastfeeding unless they are your own. Equally, a mother's diet does not give her child eczema or gas. The exception to this is the condition FPIAP discussed in Chapter 2.

Infant Formula

According to the same study as above, specialist formulas are being overprescribed despite a lack of solid evidence that they prevent cow's milk allergy. Although many guidelines for cow's milk allergy recommend using these infant formulas for prevention of the allergy, or troublesome-seeming symptoms like regurgitation (spitting up) or rashes, a review of the research behind the guidelines revealed that 81% of guideline authors recommending specialist formulas had a conflict of interest with formula manufacturers. In many cases, these recommendations end up discouraging many mums from nursing.

Having said that, if breastfeeding is genuinely not possible, infant formula can be a great option. Breast is ideal but not best. The best milk for your baby is the one they can get regularly so that they can grow and thrive.

Newer infant formulas containing human milk oligosaccharides (HMOs) may go some of the way in bridging the gap between breastmilk and formula. HMOs are short chains of indigestible sugars that make up the third biggest solid component of breastmilk after lactose and fat. They boost immune function by preventing bacteria from binding to cells and promoting a healthy balance of microorganisms in the baby's gut.

There are over 1000 known HMOs, with their composition in breastmilk varying from mother to mother and over the course of lactation. However, manufacturers have recently found ways to add the most dominant oligosaccharide, 2'-fucosyllactose (2'FL), to infant formula. Research has found that infants fed these special HMO-containing formulas had similar resilience to colds, ear infections and diarrhoea as breastfed babies.

Getting Hands On

Although caregivers do not have to avoid certain foods themselves, everyone must wash their hands after handling any foods, creams etc and before touching a baby's skin. This is especially important if the child has eczema as the broken skin can act as a gateway to trigger sensitisation and allergies as per the dual allergen exposure hypothesis.

First Reaction

Typically, an allergic reaction is not seen after the first exposure to a food as the body must first become 49ensitized. However, according to allergists, the child often has an aversion to the food before we see the allergic reaction

Chicken was my baby's first solid food. After six months of eating it safely, at age one, she had four allergic reactions to which we couldn't initially pinpoint a cause. It was as though a switch had been flipped and she became allergic to chicken. Where a reaction does occur the first time a child eats the food, as we saw with wheat, it is likely the child was 49ensitized through the skin beforehand.

Introducing Early and Often

If you are worried about allergies, it is a pretty nerve-racking thought to introduce new foods to your baby, especially those on the priority allergen list. But it is the best thing you can do to prevent allergies developing. The window of opportunity seems to be between four and eleven months of age. If your child is at risk of allergies, i.e. already has some allergies, eczema or asthma, or has ever had an anaphylactic reaction, make sure you check with your doctor before introducing any high-risk foods as she may recommend doing a skin prick test first and/or introducing the food under medical supervision.

Sibling Rivalry

Atopy runs in families but food allergies do not. Having one child with food allergies does not mean all, if any, subsequent children will also have them. In fact, there is some evidence that increasing birth order reduces the probability of developing allergies, with first-born children most likely to be allergic and subsequent kids less so.

Allergy tests are not done routinely on siblings of allergic children unless they have also exhibited signs of a reaction. The reason is two-fold:

- A false positive would mean restricting a food unnecessarily with the risk of creating an allergy.
- The first exposure to a food should be through the digestive system, not the skin.

Little Mr and Miss Fussypants

Kids with food allergies tend to be fussier eaters than those without. Our primary needs as humans – food, rest and safety – are paramount in infancy. Healthy babies are at their happiest when they are well rested and have a full stomach (and a clean diaper).

Children who develop food allergies as babies do not build a positive association with food as they have experienced pain and suffering from eating. Understandably, this leads to fussy feeding habits and a refusal to try new things. Combining this with the reduced food choices because of allergies, can lead to parents feeling frustrated, exhausted and slightly envious of other families who seem to have 'easy' kids.

When you are at your wit's end, remind yourself of the following:

- All children are difficult in their own way but some parents just don't talk about it.
- Your child isn't trying to be difficult, they just need to overcome some fear and trauma.
- This is an opportunity to build your creativity skills which you will transfer to other areas of your life.
- Many children outgrow wheat allergy so this too shall (hopefully) pass.

:: Helpful Hint: How to Introduce New Foods to a Baby's Diet

Introduce only one new food at a time, starting with a tiny amount - perhaps a quarter of a teaspoon - on the first day. You will double the amount every day for four days, introducing nothing else new in that time.

Each time you give the food in those four days, follow these steps:

1. Have one extra adult available to help in case of emergency.
2. Make sure everyone is dressed, your diaper bag and purse are packed and next to the door and your phone is charged.
3. Have your transport ready, i.e. ensure your car has fuel, baby's car seat is at hand and your keys are easily accessible.
4. Cook your chosen food either on its own - steamed or boiled - or with foods that are already established in your baby's diet.
5. Take a clear photo of the baby's face with your phone. This is for your reference when you are questioning whether a red patch was there before you started.
6. Apply a barrier ointment like petroleum jelly onto the baby's face. Infants have very delicate skin and this is to prevent irritation that might be confused for an allergic reaction, especially if there is underlying eczema.
7. Offer the child a tiny amount of the food - up to a quarter teaspoon - and note the time.
8. If it is a mealtime, continue to feed the baby the rest of their usual meal and watch for any symptoms including:
   - Flushed face, hives, rash, itchy skin
   - Itchy, runny or blocked nose
   - *Swelling of eyes, face, throat, or tongue

- *Clearing throat continuously, coughing, trouble breathing, speaking or swallowing
- *Abdominal cramps, diarrhoea, vomiting
- *Sudden faintness, paleness, or weakness as blood pressure drops

If you think you are seeing skin symptoms, take another photo and compare this with the earlier one to confirm. If symptoms do occur, note the time and head to the hospital.

If it is an emergency, i.e. the starred (*) symptoms on the list above, administer an epinephrine device if you have one and tell the other adult to call an ambulance while you monitor the child. Say, "I have a ___ year/month old having an anaphylactic reaction and need an ambulance".

If you don't see a reaction that day, offer half a teaspoon of the food the next day, following the same steps.

On day three, offer a full teaspoon, working up to two teaspoons on day four.

If you still haven't seen any symptoms, congratulations! Keep the food in the diet regularly. As our paediatric allergist used to say, "introduce early, introduce often".

Chapter 12
Dealing with Doctors

The first step when you encounter symptoms that you suspect may be an allergic reaction is to see a doctor. This may be your family doctor or an emergency room physician depending on the severity of the symptoms. The doctor will take a history and, if needed, treat the reaction. You will then be referred to a specialist in paediatrics and/or allergies. Using the tests discussed in Chapter 14 and a complete history, they will be able to confirm whether it is an allergy (involving the immune system), an intolerance (involving the gastrointestinal system but not the immune system) or neither.

Once the doctor has confirmed any allergies, you will be given a management plan. This will involve what to avoid, which medications to use (antihistamines and/or epinephrine auto-injectors) and under what circumstances. A copy of this document, often called the Anaphylaxis Action Plan, can then be given to your child's school or childcare provider.

You will be told when to return for a follow-up appointment and retests. This is often done once a year. At the appointment, you may even discuss whether oral immunotherapy is an option. We will cover all the tests – skin prick test, specific IgE blood test, oral food challenge – as well as oral immunotherapy in the following chapters.

Managing allergies, or any health condition for that matter, is a team effort, including your doctor, nurses, dieticians, and you. You need to see eye-to-eye and work together. The doctor is the expert in the disease. You are the expert in yourself and your child.

When I initially suspected that my child was allergic to chicken, I was told repeatedly by both our paediatrician and our allergist that this is not possible. What they should have said is that it is not *probable* as it is very rare, but it is theoretically possible to be allergic to any protein. Before our next allergist appointment where I knew we would be repeating skin prick tests, I steamed a small piece of chicken and took it with me to add to the tests. Our allergist did the test, perhaps to humour me, and, lo and behold, I was right.

Although a hunch is easy to dismiss, data is not. You may be an anxious, sleep-deprived, first-time parent like I was, but you may also have very valid points. It is easier to be assertive if you have facts so collect data to present to your medical team so that you can find the best solutions together.

:: Helpful Hint: Preparing for your Doctor's Appointment

Getting the right information from the right source is vitally important for both your family's safety and sanity. Having a plan that you understand and can actually follow, i.e. not too time-consuming or expensive for example, will put your mind at ease.

Before your appointments, compile the following lists on paper:

Medical history

- Dates of reactions
- Foods that were eaten
- Symptoms seen
- Timeline of what happened

Any questions, which may include:

- What should we avoid?
- Can we have a document to provide to our childcare provider or school?
- Can we get a prescription for medications and a demonstration on how to use the epinephrine auto-injector prescribed?
- What steps should we follow in an emergency?
- In case of a reaction, what medication do we use, who do we call, and when should we come back in for a review?
- What is the schedule of appointments?
- What should we do if we have questions later?

Chapter 13
What are the Alternatives?

With eczema and allergies becoming increasingly more common in the developed world, they are often seen as trivial and easy to solve. Everybody seems to have an opinion or some great advice that they heard through the grapevine. And though the advice may be well-intentioned, it may not actually be good.

The internet, in particular, is full of reports of magical tests and miraculous cures - almost guaranteed to be unproven by science. Remember, the plural of anecdote is not data. In fact, bad advice in desperate hands can be a dangerous thing.

As you may remember, life-threatening allergies are not very common at all. They are serious medical conditions that are still being researched by specialists in the field.

Nonetheless, there are a plethora of tests claiming to diagnose food allergies. Most of these have not been proven by science to work. Those that have been tested, have been shown to have no value. Below are a few examples:

- Electrodermal or Vega Test: A mixture of homeopathy and acupuncture, this has been debunked in scientific studies. The patient holds the suspect food in one hand while the electrical resistance is measured across the skin. In reality, there is no difference between people with allergies and those without.

- Applied Kinesiology: This test is based on the premise that if you are allergic to something, holding it will weaken your muscles. Like in the previous test, the patient will hold a container of the allergen, e.g. a glass of milk, in one hand while the practitioner tests the strength in the other arm. Not only is this preposterous, it is very easily influenced by external factors.

- Nambudripad's Allergy Elimination Technique (NAET): Similar to applied kinesiology, this test asserts that holding an allergen will block energy channels which can then be relieved using acupuncture.

- Hair Analysis: A sample of the patient's hair is sent to a laboratory for analysis, with claims that the presence or absence of specific minerals indicates food allergies and sensitivities. Hair is not involved in allergic reactions at all.

- IgG Antibody Test: This is a blood test that measures the total level of IgG antibodies specific to certain foods. Sometimes called the York test, this is usually marketed as a 'food sensitivity test', and always reveals a long list of 'allergens' much to the patient's horror and delight (we all want concrete answers to our symptoms).

    I once met someone who was avoiding 82 items following her York Test. The length of this list is not surprising as everyone forms IgG antibodies to anything that is not *self* i.e. human, making the list solely a reflection of what someone has eaten over their life. Although two specific types of IgG antibodies (IgG1 and IgG4) are involved as allergies develop and resolve, the level of total IgG in the blood doesn't indicate anything.

Sadly, this is not a comprehensive list of bogus tests. There are many more where these came from and the National Institute for Health and Care Excellence (NICE) has a list of tests that should not be used to diagnose allergies.

Of course, alternative medicine has its place. There has been research to show that Traditional Chinese Medicine (TCM) and

Ayurveda can have promising results in many health conditions. In fact, in 2012, a medicine based on nine traditional Chinese herbs named Food Allergy Herbal Formula 2 (FAHF-2) was able to block peanut-induced anaphylaxis in trials with mice. This gave hope for an alternative approach to managing food allergies. However, trials in humans in 2015 were not as successful. After six months of treatment, FAHF-2 was found to have no effect in improving tolerance to food allergens.

Alternative medicine practitioners themselves can be wary of using traditional treatments. I once asked a TCM doctor, whose father and grandfather were also well-known TCM doctors, whether she used herbal treatments and traditional tests on her peanut and egg-allergic child. Her answer was a vehement "no". She said that even if they were effective, which they have not yet been proven to be, the concoctions would be too bitter for children so there would be no adherence to a course of treatment.

In general, a blanket skepticism for all things conventional could be very dangerous in the case of allergies where there is no evidence that alternative medicine works. If you are still not convinced that conventional Western medicine is the way to go, ask yourself whether in the event of a medical emergency like a heart attack or anaphylactic shock, you would call an ambulance and head to the nearest hospital, or call your acupuncturist.

Chapter 14
Testing, Testing 123

Although there are many tests claiming to diagnose allergies, only two have been proven to be clinically valid by specialists in the field. These are the skin prick test and the ImmunoCap blood tests. The tests all measure Immunoglobulin E (IgE) antibodies which drive allergic reactions. Interpretation of the test results takes the specialist knowledge of an experienced board-certified allergist as the numbers are not clear cut and must be combined with the patient's history.

Skin Prick Test

The skin prick test (SPT) uses a liquid solution containing the allergen on the skin to detect the level of IgE antibodies present. Multiple allergens can be tested at the same time.

The doctor or nurse will decide on a list of allergens and assign each a number. They will then mark these numbers on the forearm with a pen and place a drop of each solution next to the corresponding number. Each dot will then be gently pricked with a small lancet (a needle that resembles a tiny chip fork). There will be two extra pricks. They are the controls, saline and histamine.

After 10 minutes, the forearm will be checked for red raised domes called hives, wheals or *urticaria*. The allergist or nurse will measure the size of each hive in millimetres (mm). The size shows the likelihood of allergy and not necessarily the severity. The saline prick is the negative control and should have no reaction. If it does, then any other hives that come up during this test could be from just scratching the skin, as in the case of dermographism. Histamine is the positive control. It shows that the skin can react and the size of the wheal from this prick is used as a reference for all the tests. A skin prick test to an allergen should in theory be at least 3mm bigger than the histamine control to be considered positive.

A positive test shows a 50% probability of allergy to this protein. A false positive could be due to:

- **Cross reaction**: This is where the proteins in one substance are so similar to those in another one that if a person is allergic to one, they may have a positive skin prick test to the other despite not actually being allergic to both. Examples include tree nuts and tree pollen, or peanuts and lentils.
- **Reactive skin**: If a person has active eczema flares, their skin tends to be more reactive to any physical or chemical irritation. This is also the case for someone with chronic hives. The skin may then show a reaction even if there was no allergy. However, the saline control prick would also show a reaction, indicating that the results may not be reliable.

A false negative reaction could be because

- the test solution does not have enough extract.
- the body has never had exposure to the protein, e.g. for a baby, and so has not formed IgE antibodies yet.

As you can imagine, antihistamine medications can skew results by suppressing reactions and so must be avoided for at least two days before skin prick tests.

Blood Tests

If allergies were not ruled out using the skin prick tests combined with a patient history, blood tests will be done. These measure the level of IgE antibodies in the blood that are specific to the proteins (allergens) in question and are a better predictor of what will happen if the patient eats the food. The more allergen-

60

specific IgE (sIgE) there is in the blood, the more there is likely to be on special cells central to allergic reactions called *mast cells*.

The standard blood test to diagnose allergies used to be the radioallergosorbent test (RAST) but this has been largely replaced by the newer ImmunoCap test which is more specific. The units for this test are kU/L (kilo units per litre) or kuA/L where 'A' stands for 'allergen-specific'.

Multiple allergens can be tested at the same time and in fact, if it is relevant, component testing might also be done to see which parts of the allergen are causing the reaction in the individual. For example, the protein omega-5-gliadin in gluten is the most frequent trigger of wheat-dependent exercise-induced anaphylaxis and may be responsible for more severe reactions in some people.

In addition to being useful for the initial diagnosis, this blood test can indicate the course of the allergy over time. The allergen-specific IgE levels are checked regularly, usually once a year, to see if they have changed. If levels start to drop considerably and consistently, it may indicate that the person is starting to outgrow the allergy.

A positive specific IgE (sIgE) test confirms sensitisation but does not necessarily mean a person is allergic to that protein. Many people have high sIgE numbers and have never had a reaction. Others who were once allergic, may continue to have high sIgE levels to the allergen even after they outgrow the allergy and can tolerate the substance.

For wheat, the peak sIgE can be a good predictor of how long the allergy will persist, but studies have shown that in many cases those with even the highest levels go on to outgrow wheat allergy. Compared with the blood test for other common food allergens, sIgE cut-off levels for wheat are not as accurate at predicting what will happen if an allergic person eats a wheat-containing food. This is where the Oral Food Challenge, covered in the next chapter, can be useful.

:: Helpful Hint: How to Make Blood Tests Easier

Blood tests are never fun, even if you don't have a fear of needles. Below are some ways to make them go more smoothly.

- <u>Drink up</u> - Arrive well hydrated so that your veins are plump and your blood is more runny. Drawing blood will be quicker and easier.

- <u>At arm's length</u> - Wear a short sleeved top to make access to your arm easier. The less time and energy spent fumbling around, the smoother the experience.

- <u>Warm and cuddly</u> - Wear at least one layer on top of your short-sleeved outfit just before the test to make sure you are warm. The toastier the better, without getting so hot you are flustered and annoyed. When you are warm, your blood vessels are less constricted and closer to the skin surface meaning less time and pain digging around looking for a vein.

- <u>Walk</u> - Another way to expand your veins and bring them closer to the skin surface is exercise. You can walk around before the test (or better yet, walk all the way there). In the case of young children, let them run around and play. This will calm nerves as well.

- <u>Feeling numb</u> - If you are worried about pain, call ahead and ask whether you can bring some over-the-counter numbing cream (they may provide it) and how it can fit into the phlebotomist's preferred routine. The cream is usually applied to the elbow creases 30 minutes before the blood test, if needed.

Here are some extra tips for parents of young children:

- <u>Straddle</u> - For a young child, the best position to do the blood test might be sitting face-to-face on a parent's lap, in a secure hug. Mum or dad can comfort the child, hold them still, and direct their gaze away from the needle.

- <u>Superpowers</u> - We told our daughter that the procedure was a way to get superpowers. Yes, it would be painful, we said, but she'd be able to run faster and jump higher afterwards. We would ask her to do a jump after the blood test and make a huge fuss over her new impressive skills. Every time we needed to have another set of blood tests, we were "topping up the superpowers".

- <u>Bribery</u> - If the promise of superpowers isn't enough, there's always good old-fashioned bribery. Bring along a shiny new toy/book/hairband that you know your child would love, hidden in a bag. Give this to your little one after the blood test as though it came from the phlebotomist. Although you won't get the credit, it will make your life easier in the long run as your child might even look forward to their next blood test.

Chapter 15
Oral Food Challenge

The absolute best way to determine presence or absence of allergy is to reproduce a reaction, if any. When other tests have not come back conclusively positive, and there is no history of anaphylaxis to the suspected allergen, an oral food challenge (OFC) can either prove there is an allergy or rule it out completely. This makes the oral food challenge the gold standard of allergy testing.

A challenge is also useful when we think the person may have outgrown the allergy - based on lower specific IgE levels in the blood and smaller skin prick tests - and we are considering reintroducing the food into the diet. In this case, the OFC helps to 'delabel' the patient as allergic to that food.

In an OFC, food containing the suspected allergen is eaten, in controlled doses, under the watchful eye of medical experts. The full dose will depend on the food and its protein content. Remember, the body reacts to protein in the food. If the challenge is successful and the patient is able to consume the full dose, they are said to have 'passed the food challenge'. If an allergic reaction occurs at any stage of the OFC, the challenge was 'failed'.

Despite wheat being one of the most prevalent food allergens, there are very few published studies assessing the risk of anaphylaxis during a challenge to wheat. There is much more information on other allergens like peanut, milk, egg and soy. However, it has been shown that:

- When blood tests show higher levels of specific IgE to wheat there is a higher likelihood of a reaction during an OFC (i.e. a failed challenge) but the reaction may or may not be severe. Blood tests cannot predict the severity of reactions particularly for wheat.

- There are likely many different parts (epitopes) of wheat proteins to which specific IgE can be formed and this is likely why we see different types of wheat allergy.

- Younger children can react to smaller amounts of wheat so starting small (well below 100mg) in an oral food challenge is prudent. For reference, a slice of white bread typically contains around 2000mg (2g) of wheat protein.

Although they are considered safe for the most part, up to 28% of oral food challenges have systemic reactions. An OFC is therefore often done in a hospital, with a team of medical staff - doctors, nurses and dieticians - monitoring a few patients at a time. It can have significant costs in terms of risk and time so the decision to carry out a challenge is not taken lightly. However it may be worthwhile.

A review by specialists at National Jewish Health in Colorado looking at over 100 children with positive allergy blood tests, found that 93% of foods being avoided could actually be tolerated in an oral food challenge. Even patients with a previous reaction to the food, were able to tolerate it, with 84% passing their OFC. This meant that nearly all the foods were being unnecessarily avoided and could be reintroduced to the diets of the patients.

Weighing Up Risks and Benefits

For us, passing a challenge, especially to wheat, meant an enormous improvement in our family's quality of life. However, we did need to balance the potential benefits with the risks involved each time we were given the opportunity to have a challenge.

Before deciding whether to undergo an oral food challenge, discuss the following questions with your family and your doctor:

- What will be gained from doing a challenge? How will it help?
- What is the family's risk tolerance? Is this aligned with that of the doctor?
- What is the procedure if a reaction occurs? If it needs to be treated as an emergency with epinephrine, will everyone be completely traumatised?
- What is the added nutritional value of the food being tested? For someone with multiple food allergies whose diet is very restricted, adding in one food group like dairy could be significant.
- If there is also asthma or uncontrolled eczema, is this an additional risk? Is there help available to bring these under control?

The chance of an anaphylactic reaction during an OFC is very real, particularly with wheat. In July 2017, a three-year old American boy died during a baked milk oral food challenge. It was the first, and only, reported death from an OFC but serves as a stark reminder of the risk of fatal anaphylaxis.

We started on our allergy journey in 2015 so had had multiple challenges, including a few failed ones, before hearing this tragic news. These were horrible experiences all around as we had effectively induced an allergic reaction in our baby. We watched our child suffering, knowing that it was due to completely avoidable decisions that we had made. After three instances of anaphylaxis from failed challenges (to dairy and wheat), we realised our risk tolerance was not aligned with that of our doctor. We had a frank and honest conversation and, as they say, the rest is history. We climbed the milk and egg ladders, and successfully completed oral immunotherapy (covered in the next chapter) for wheat, under the guidance of our wonderful allergist. Our lives are forever changed.

In general, if a doctor thinks the patient will not pass an oral food challenge, they will not agree to it. Equally, parents, particularly mothers, know their child best. If you feel quite certain that your child will not pass an OFC based on previous exposure, don't do it yet. On the other hand, if the doctor suggests a challenge and, after discussing all your concerns and weighing up the risks and benefits, you both think there is a high enough chance your child might pass it, seriously consider proceeding (perhaps slowly in smaller increments). The improvement in your physical and mental health could be worth it.

What Happens at an OFC Appointment?

You will be told ahead of time what food to bring and in what quantity. Aim to bring at least 50% more than the requested amount in case some of it ends up on the floor or elsewhere. For a wheat challenge, the easiest foods are pastas and breads that contain few ingredients, and ideally no eggs. This makes it easier to calculate the amount of wheat protein in each dose.

Food challenge appointments are usually four hours long, giving time for the health checks at the start and end, administering the doses, and monitoring for an hour at the end. They are often set for early in the morning.

1. You will talk through the process and sign a consent form.
2. The patient's height and weight will be measured so that the right dose of medication can be given if needed.
3. Their 'vitals' (blood pressure, heart rate, and blood oxygen level) will be checked as a baseline for the day. The heart rate and blood pressure will likely be slightly elevated due to nerves.
4. The doctor or nurse will listen to the patient's chest and look at their skin for any eczema flares or redness before starting.
5. The full dose will be broken down into four to eight steps. The first will be tiny and each subsequent dose will be at least double the amount of the previous one. The steps will be 15-20 minutes apart.
6. Before each successive dose, the blood pressure, heart rate and blood oxygen level will be checked again.

7. At the first sign of a reaction, the challenge will be stopped and the reaction will be treated.
8. If there is no reaction after the final dose, the patient will wait for an hour in the ward before being discharged with instructions on how to maintain the food in the diet regularly (and likely a huge sigh of relief from everyone!).

:: Helpful Hint: How to Prepare for your Oral Food Challenge

- Refer to the section on co-factors that can cause bigger reactions (:: Helpful Hint: How Much Causes a Reaction?) to make sure you are not putting yourself at additional risk.

- Bring 50% more of the food being challenged as accidents can and may well happen and food may end up on the floor, in your bag etc.

- If possible, bring one extra adult to the appointment or have them wait nearby.

- Make sure your phone, tablet etc are all fully charged. I normally don't condone copious amounts of screen-time but this is a special circumstance.

- The patient must have enough of an appetite to consume the doses but not be so hungry and upset that they don't want to cooperate. If you have children, you know what I mean. A good strategy would be to offer half the usual breakfast before leaving the house for a morning OFC appointment.

- Appointments are usually four hours long so bring entertainment and activities for everyone, including yourself. This could include reading books, a sketch pad, art supplies, playdough, and crafts. If all else fails, there are always games and television shows on a phone or tablet.

- Make sure everyone, including you, is wearing comfortable clothes and shoes.

- Bring spare clothes, including underwear, in case of spills or vomiting.

- As with introducing any new foods at home, take a clear picture of the face before starting, i.e. before the first dose.

- Bring pasta sauce, honey, jam, chocolate sauce, jam, ketchup and / or any condiments that you think might help make the challenge progress when the doses get bigger and it feels like too much.

- Bring extra snacks and drinks for everyone, and if the appointment straddles a mealtime e.g. lunch, bring a small packed lunch.

Chapter 16
Oral Immunotherapy

Immunotherapy is a potential treatment for allergies that uses gradually increasing amounts of the allergen to train the body to tolerate it. Of the four different modes of immunotherapy - sublingual (tablet under the tongue), subcutaneous (allergy shots under the skin), epicutaneous (allergy patch on the skin) and oral (eating/drinking the allergen), oral immunotherapy has been shown to be the most effective for food allergies.

In the case of oral immunotherapy (OIT), the patient eats a small amount of the allergen-containing food under medical supervision, just as in an oral food challenge. This is the 'rush' phase. If there is no reaction, the patient continues to consume this dose daily at home. This phase is called 'maintenance'. At each subsequent OIT appointment, the dose is increased (called 'up-dosing') with the goal of eventually being able to tolerate a certain amount of the allergen without reaction. This final amount must be consumed on a regular basis - most likely daily, but at least three times a week - as 'maintenance' continues.

Oral immunotherapy can have astounding results. In 2014, a clinical trial called STOP II was done in Cambridge, UK. It divided 7-16 year-olds with peanut allergy into two groups. One was told to avoid peanuts altogether. The other group was given gradually increasing doses of peanut flour until the subjects were eating up to 800mg daily. For reference, a peanut is roughly 250mg. After six months of immunotherapy, 84-91% of the children were able to tolerate the equivalent of five peanuts, i.e. at least 25 times the amount of peanut protein as before starting immunotherapy.

However, OIT does not work for everyone and, in cases where it does work, the mechanisms behind it are not clear. It has also not been established whether, when it is successful, how long the tolerance will actually last. This means that OIT to treat food allergies is still considered experimental. As with oral food challenges, oral immunotherapy also carries real risks. In fact each OIT appointment is effectively like an oral food challenge, with the risk of anaphylaxis every time.

If oral immunotherapy does work, there are two possible positive outcomes:

- **Desensitisation**: This increases the threshold level of the allergen that a person can eat without having a reaction. However desensitisation is reversible. If the patient stops the maintenance phase, i.e. consuming the agreed dose several times a week, they may become allergic again. This can be seen as soon as a week after stopping treatment.

- **Tolerance**: This is when the immune system stops reacting to the protein, i.e. the person can have as much of the food as they would like without a reaction. Tolerance even when one hasn't continued consuming the daily maintenance dose is called 'sustained unresponsiveness'. This was demonstrated in the LEAP study (discussed in Chapter 7) with peanuts but, as oral immunotherapy is still relatively new, it is yet to be seen whether the tolerance is lifelong.

The dosages used for each phase of OIT are not yet clearly defined and vary considerably between published studies and in practice. Many trials aim for an end goal of 4g (4000mg) of protein per day. A mathematical modelling study hypothesised that those who can tolerate 30mg (0.03g) of a food protein should be safe from cross-contamination. This is where the food being consumed does not directly contain the allergen but is contaminated by tiny amounts from a nearby food. According to the same study, once someone can tolerate 300mg (0.3g), they could be fine in the event of accidental exposure, i.e. mistakenly eating some of their allergen.

It is unclear how and why oral immunotherapy works for some people and not others, and there is ongoing research into this. From conversations with allergists, it seems that OIT quite likely makes use of the fact that the person is outgrowing the allergy naturally and builds on that. If true, this means that immunotherapy uses the plasticity of the immune system as it matures to train the body not to overreact.

More immunotherapy studies have been done on peanuts than any other allergen, with dairy OIT research a close second. This makes peanuts and milk the best candidates at present for OIT. The US regulating authorities recently even approved a peanut OIT pill. Palforzia, manufactured by Aimmune, uses a rush dose of 12mg of peanut protein and, over the course of 12 up-dosing appointments, aims for a final daily maintenance dose of 300mg. The company is already working on a similar pill for egg and tree nut oral immunotherapy but the approval of this first drug will undoubtedly spur other pharmaceutical firms into the market, along with drugs and research into other allergens including wheat.

For now, information on wheat immunotherapy is lacking. Although there have been several small clinical trials for wheat OIT, there has only been one large (multicenter, double-blind, randomised controlled) trial to determine the safety and efficacy of wheat OIT. This was still with only 46 patients. Research into immunotherapy for wheat is continuing and should reveal protocols for treatment in the not-too-distant future. In the meantime, here is what we know:

- It is important to stay consistent with the food being used for wheat oral immunotherapy as protein content varies between different foods e.g. pasta, bread, semolina pudding etc.

- Picking the right timing for the daily OIT dose is important, particularly for wheat, as exercise must be avoided for a few hours after treatment and the person should be able to be monitored (i.e. not in a school playground).

- OIT increases the levels of the antibody IgG4 specific to the allergen. This helps the body see it as 'friend' instead of 'foe'. Meanwhile IgG1 levels tend to drop. As you may remember, IgG antibodies are a record of what you have eaten over your life. IgG1 and IgG4 are subtypes of IgG antibodies.

- Blood levels of IgE specific to the protein can remain high even after tolerance has been reached, and consequently skin prick tests often continue to be positive even though the person can consume the food safely.

- The younger the patient, the more likely that immunotherapy will be effective. This is because the immune system is more malleable at a young age and there is less IgE to different parts (epitopes) of the allergen.

-

- The longer the duration of immunotherapy, and the less breaks, the more likely it is to bring about tolerance. The benchmark so far from wheat OIT clinical trials seems to be two   years.

- Lifelong maintenance, where the food protein is consumed regularly, may be necessary to remain unresponsive to the allergen.

- Using specific probiotics and biologic agents, like lactobacillus rhamnosus and omalizumab or dupilumab, alongside OIT may boost the effectiveness of immunotherapy.

:: Helpful Hint: Is Oral Immunotherapy Right For You?

If you are thinking of embarking on a (potentially lifelong) course of oral immunotherapy, here are some factors to consider:

- **Communication**: The person having OIT must be able to verbalise if they are feeling symptoms. For pollen immunotherapy for example, a rule of thumb used by allergist Dr Anne Ellis from Queen's University in Canada is to wait until the child is at least five years old. However, we know that OIT is more effective if done early, so assess your child's verbal skills and self-awareness with your doctor.

- **Time**: It can be very time consuming to keep up with appointments which are both regular and frequent. A friend of mine ended up giving up her career as a dentist while her child was doing peanut OIT. Ask yourself whether your family can commit to this schedule at this time.

- **Fit**: Finding the right fit with the right doctor can be challenging. As it is not proven and has significant risks, many doctors are not willing to do OIT. On the other hand, some doctors can be such ardent believers in the therapy that they move too fast and this may not match your risk tolerance.

- **Risk of reactions**: OIT is effectively like doing an oral food challenge on a regular basis, with the same significant risk of anaphylaxis each time. There were multiple occasions where my child did have a reaction. Once, I am horrified to admit, I admonished her for coughing openly and not into her sleeve as she had been taught, not realising she was starting to go into anaphylaxis!

- **Commitment**: The person will need to eat the food religiously, every single day until they build some tolerance, and then most likely keep it in their diet at least two to three times a week for the rest of their life.

- **Limited information**: There is still not enough data for allergens apart from peanut and dairy, and that too has not been fully proven. We climbed the milk and egg ladders with our allergist and started immunotherapy for wheat. Although my child eventually overcame all three allergies, the road was very bumpy, with reactions along the way. OIT gave us confidence against cross-contamination and did increasingly open up her diet but I am not sure I would follow the same path again.

Chapter 17
Treating a Reaction

An allergic reaction does not look the same every time - even in the same person, exposed to the exact same allergen. This is why it is important to know all the possible symptoms (and why I have repeated them several times throughout this book!).

Symptoms of an allergic reaction tend to be seen in the body systems belonging to the heart, lungs, stomach and skin:
- Flushed face, hives, rash, red and itchy skin
- Swelling of eyes, face, throat, tongue
- Itchy, runny or blocked nose
- Clearing the throat constantly, coughing, trouble breathing/speaking/swallowing
- Stomach cramps, diarrhoea, vomiting
- Drop in blood pressure, rapid heartbeat, faintness, paleness, weakness, feeling 'floppy'. loss of consciousness
- Anxiety, distress, sense of doom

There are two main medications used to treat an allergic reaction - epinephrine (also known as adrenaline) and antihistamine.

Epinephrine

Epinephrine is a chemical messenger (hormone and neurotransmitter) that is produced in the adrenal glands. The prefix *epi* means above, and *nephros* refers to the kidney, and so *epinephrine* gets its name from the location of the adrenals. It is also known as adrenaline.

Injecting epinephrine into a muscle (intramuscular) is the first-line defence against an allergic reaction. It is the preferred choice because it works fast, preventing mast cells from releasing their chemical contents (degranulating) and stopping a reaction in its tracks. The effects can be seen in just a few minutes. I have seen this in action and it is truly amazing.

Epinephrine already circulates in the body, rising and falling at different times depending on many factors. The issue is that during an allergic reaction, the level may not ramp up fast enough to protect the body. This is why anyone diagnosed with IgE-mediated allergies must carry an epinephrine auto-injector (EAI) at all times. EAIs are also sometimes called adrenaline auto-injectors (AAI). 'Auto' means 'self' so this is a device which allows someone to inject themselves with adrenaline.

There are many brands of EAIs available like Emerade or Auvi-Q but EpiPen, manufactured by Mylar, dominates the market. As a result, 'EpiPen' is often used to mean any EAI, just the way 'Hoover' is used colloquially in Britain to mean vacuum cleaner.

There are generally two dosages in EAIs - the one for children contains half the epinephrine of the one for adults, i.e. 0.15mg vs 0.30mg. Check with your doctor when it is time for your child to switch over to the adult device. This is usually when they reach around 25 to 30 kg in weight.

Multiple studies have shown that epinephrine is not used as often as it should be during allergic reactions. Possible reasons people hesitate to use it are a fear of the unfamiliar, fear of pain or injury from the needle and a reluctance to waste money and time in the hospital. However, timely use of an EAI saves lives.

EpiPen's catchy slogan helps you remember how to use the device (and is helpful for other devices too):

"Blue to the sky. Orange to the thigh"

This refers to holding the device in your dominant hand, removing the safety cap (which is blue for EpiPens), and then swinging your arm down to push the needle side (orange in EpiPens) into the outer thigh.

You must hold the device in place for three to five seconds to allow all the medication to penetrate. Although the advice used to be ten seconds, doctors realised that the risk of a distressed patient, especially a child, moving while the needle is inside and bending it, was not worth the incremental, if any, increase in medication.

Get a refresher session on how to use your EAI from your doctor or pharmacist as often as you need. You can also refer to the manufacturer's website for videos whenever required, as well as order training devices so that you can practise and train others. Do this until it is second nature so that you feel more confident in an emergency.

Epinephrine causes the 'fight or flight' response in the body. This can be quite a disconcerting experience, especially as the feelings come on so suddenly. In the course of ramping up breathing and circulation, the boost in epinephrine will make the person feel anxious, make their heart start pounding and their face feel flushed. It will make them want to get up and move but they must stay sitting or, ideally, lying down until the paramedics arrive as getting up can cause a sudden drop in blood pressure and even cardiac arrest.

Here are some more things to remember:

- An allergic person must have two epinephrine autoinjectors with them at all times. It has never failed to amaze me how few people carry theirs on playdates. Out of interest, I often ask other allergy families if they have their EAI and not once have   I   heard   "yes"!

- The EAI must be injected into the outer thigh. This ensures it doesn't hit a vein but still delivers sufficient medication to the   body   in   a   timely   manner.

- In an absolute emergency, for example where you cannot breathe and every second counts, you can use the EAI through light clothing (like cotton leggings, but not through thick seams, buttons, zips etc).

- Note the time when you used the auto-injector. If symptoms are not getting better after five to ten minutes, you may need to use a second device.

- Always call an ambulance and say "I have a x-year old with anaphylaxis". If it is a child, make sure to state this.

- As EAIs tend to have a shelf life of roughly one year, set a reminder on your calendar and your phone to refill your prescription.

- Auto-injectors must be stored between 15° and 30°C so do not leave them in a car.

- Check the window on the side of the device regularly to make sure the liquid is clear with no cloudy floating bits (precipitates).

Although in an ideal situation you would always use in-date medication, the research has shown that an expired epinephrine auto-injector is better than nothing. As long as the liquid doesn't look discoloured, cloudy or have any precipitates (bits) floating in it, studies have found EpiPens to be safe even years after their printed expiry date. The epinephrine concentration can start to drop after the expiry date but studies have found that even 24 months after the expiry date printed on the side, most EpiPens still had 90% of their epinephrine concentration. Anaphylaxis is a life-threatening emergency and any boost of epinephrine is better than none. If an expired device is all you have to hand and it looks clear, use it. Then call an ambulance as you would normally.

What happens in the hospital?

Anaphylaxis is treated in the emergency department of the hospital. Because of the risk of a 'rebound reaction' the patient is monitored for four hours after the reaction, even if the EAI worked and they feel fine. For much of the time, the patient may be hooked up to heart rate and blood oxygen monitors.

If symptoms of the reaction have not fully subsided, the patient may also be given intravenous epinephrine and fluids, and/or antihistamines along with other drugs like steroids to boost the effect of epinephrine and antihistamines.

Once given the all clear, the patient will be discharged with a prescription for more auto-injectors and some instructions on whether to take antihistamines in the next 24 hours. Once home, you must update your allergist or family doctor in case they think it is necessary to book in a review.

Antihistamines

During an allergic reaction, histamine released from mast cells causes blood vessels to expand and become leakier, and the skin to become hot, red, itchy and swollen. Antihistamines block the action of histamine and stop its effects on the body.

Some doctors, particularly in Canada, hesitate to recommend antihistamines as treatment for an allergic reaction as having both an epinephrine auto-injector and an antihistamine as part of a patient's Anaphylaxis Action Plan can cause confusion on which one to use. People, including emergency room medics, tend to go for the more familiar option - an oral medication - even when they should have used epinephrine. As you can imagine, this can have disastrous outcomes.

Antihistamines take much longer than epinephrine to work. It can take between 60 and 180 minutes for an antihistamine to reach its maximum concentration in the blood, compared to less than ten minutes with intramuscular epinephrine. Antihistamines can also mask some symptoms making it harder to recognise that any subsequent symptoms, like coughing or vomiting, are not part of something new but in fact the involvement of a second or third body system - i.e. anaphylaxis.

The Diphenhydramine Debacle

It turns out that some of the best-known and widely-used antihistamines are the least safe. Medications like diphenhydramine (Benadryl), hydroxyzine (Atarax) and chlorphenamine (Piriton, Allercalm) pass the blood-brain barrier causing drowsiness, respiratory depression (slower, less effective breathing), and impaired concentration and memory. The effect is like sedation and the drugs have been found to result in fatalities from motor vehicle accidents, overdoses and even sudden cardiac arrest.

A randomised controlled trial comparing the effect of diphenhydramine (first-generation antihistamine), fexofenadine (second-generation antihistamine), alcohol and placebo found that driving performance was worst after using diphenhydramine. Performance with the common over-the-counter drug was actually worse than with a blood alcohol concentration of 0.1%, well above legal drink driving limits in any country! Drowsiness ratings were not able to predict the level of impairment to cognitive and motor skills showing that in many cases people are putting themselves and others at serious risk.

Second- and third-generation antihistamines which were developed later, do not pass the blood-brain barrier yet are just as, if not more, effective. Although people often feel like older antihistamines work fast, that feeling is often just the side effects kicking in. Studies have found that to have the same outcome against histamine's effects, diphenhydramine (Benadryl) took 79.2 minutes compared to 50 minutes with cetirizine (a second-generation antihistamine). Some other examples of next-generation antihistamines are desloratadine and fexofenadine. Some drugs like rupatidine (Rupall) even block other chemicals involved in the allergic response like platelet-activating factor.

However, since first-generation antihistamines are so easily available and have been around for so long (Benadryl has been on the market since 1946), many people use them as though they are completely benign. Some even use them daily as a sleep aid, especially on children with severe eczema who have trouble sleeping. I was advised to do this by my paediatrician many years ago but didn't feel comfortable with the idea.

I am now grateful I followed my gut. According to the Canadian Society of Allergy and Clinical Immunology (CSACI), Benadryl would not pass the safety standards in place today. In 2019, the CSACI recommended that first-generation antihistamines only be used if absolutely necessary and eventually not be available over the counter.

In any case, when choosing an antihistamine, bear in mind that a suspension (liquid) will work fastest as the body does not have to break down the coating on a tablet. It may therefore be worth using a liquid medication even for adults.

:: Helpful Hint: How to Give Medicine to a Baby or Toddler

Whether antihistamines, antibiotics, anti-reflux drugs, there may be times when you need to administer medication to a young child. The following steps will help:

1. Measure the correct dose into the syringe.
2. Cradle the baby in your lap if you can, with their head slightly elevated.
3. Put the tip of the syringe into the corner crease of their mouth, along the inside of the cheek, not in the centre. Putting the syringe in the centre of the lips will make the medicine hit the back of their throat and can cause choking.
4. Press the plunger of the syringe gently to administer 0.5-1ml of liquid.
5. Blow gently but quickly onto the child's face. This will induce their reflex to swallow.
6. Let the child catch their breath if needed and then repeat until you've given the full dose.

Chapter 18
Looking at Labels

If there was ever a time to become a label junkie, this would be it. When you have food allergies in the family, knowing exactly what is in your food, cosmetics and immediate surroundings is imperative.

Always read ingredient labels, even of products you buy regularly, as companies do change their recipes. Avoid things that do not have a label, like open containers in delicatessens or restaurant buffets.

Below is the method I have developed to save time when reading labels. It is split into three steps. As most foods don't make the cut after the first step, it saves me reading a long list of boring ingredients several times a day.

1. Look at the bottom of the ingredient list to see there is an allergy warning like "contains/may contain".
2. If the food passes the above test, scan every line of the ingredient list. Sometimes common allergens are highlighted in bold.
3. If you haven't discounted the item already for having your allergen, read every ingredient, one by one for any warning bells.
4. If you are not sure about an ingredient, do not use the product.

Examples of wheat products to skip:

-   Bread containing any wheat
-   Bread crumbs

- Breakfast cereals and cereal bars
- Pasta
- Wheat bran, wheat grass, wheat starch, wheat berries, wheat protein
- Baked goods like muffins, cakes, biscuits, cookies, crackers, donuts
- Breaded or battered foods e.g. chicken nuggets, fish fingers etc
- Croutons
- Wafers, ice cream cones

There are some foods that sound like they contain wheat but are actually safe. Glutinous rice used in Asian cooking does not contain gluten. Instead, the name refers to the sticky, gluey consistency of this variety of rice when it is cooked. Buckwheat is not a form of wheat. It is not even a cereal but in fact the seed of a fruit, more closely related to rhubarb than wheat. Both glutinous rice and buckwheat are gluten-free.

On the other hand, not all foods containing wheat are obvious. Texturised wheat gluten can mimic the appearance and consistency of chicken, pork or beef, making wheat protein one of the most commonly used plant proteins, along with soy, to be used both in meat products and as a meat substitute.

In addition, regular oats are generally cross-contaminated with wheat as farmers alternate between the two crops on the same patch of land in the interest of soil health. 'Gluten-free' oats will have been grown on dedicated fields making them safe for wheat allergy sufferers.

Here are some more examples of wheat-containing foods to avoid:

- Bulgur
- Couscous
- Matzo
- Farina

- Farro
- Einkorn
- Emmer
- Kamut
- Spelt
- Semolina
- Seitan
- Oats or oat milk (unless labelled 'gluten-free')
- Malt
- Ale, beer
- Ice cream cones
- Soya sauce

When reading ingredient labels, look out for the following:

- Hydrolysed wheat protein, hydrolysed vegetable protein
- Starch e.g. Modified food starch, modified vegetable starch etc
- Triticale and anything that contains the word 'triticum'
- Durum

These can often be found in the following products:

- Dressings, sauces, marinades, gravies
- Processed meats e.g. canned or deli
- Plant-based meat substitutes i.e. vegan 'chicken' etc
- Soups
- Surimi
- Vegetable gums
- Stock cubes
- Hot dogs, burger patties

Stricter laws to protect people with food allergies mean that manufacturers sometimes over-label their products. They add a statement on the foods saying they "may contain" a long list of allergens in order to cover their backs when in reality the food could be perfectly safe from most of the allergens listed. This practice leads to already restricted diets becoming even more limited. Doctors and dieticians are working with the food industry to strike the right balance. In the meantime, it is better to be safe than sorry. Over-labelling trumps under-labelling any day.

Non-Food Sources of Wheat

Personal care products like creams, soaps, shampoos and cosmetics sometimes contain wheat in the form of hydrolysed wheat protein or traces of it. Skin moisturisers, particularly for eczema, often contain oats to relieve itching. However, these oats are not gluten-free so can cause reactions in those allergic to wheat. My daughter would break out in giant hives within minutes of using certain creams until I figured out the link.

Some higher-end lipsticks, mascaras and hair care products contain wheat for it's lubricating properties or as a binder. The ingredient list will list wheat germ or triticum vulgare, but also keep an eye out for any of the other names in the list above.

Modelling compounds for young children, like PlayDoh, are made primarily from wheat. It is a staple in many daycares and homes. For those with severe wheat allergy, ask for it to be eliminated completely as children will touch many other surfaces after playing with it leaving traces of wheat everywhere. Instead, consider making your own gluten-free playdough using the recipe on the next page.

Sometimes wheat is not in the products we put in our bodies or on them. 'Harvest' wreaths used in home decorations, particularly in the autumn, often feature wheat or wheat-berries. If you are unsure of what something contains, steer clear of it.

:: Helpful Hint: Gluten-Free Playdough Recipe

For nearly four years, until we started oral immunotherapy for wheat, playdough was my nemesis. We avoided the stuff at all cost. After a few unpleasant experiences, this also meant avoiding playgroups and daycare centres that insisted on using wheat-based playdough (i.e. most of them). And then I found a recipe for gluten-free playdough that was easy and quick, using ingredients I already had in my cupboards.

One batch of the temptingly colourful, wonderfully mushy and, most importantly, non-lethal stuff offers hours* of quiet fun for my kids – a very welcome event for any parent! You can even ask for your daycare provider to switch to this recipe or offer to make it for them, as I did.

Ingredients (makes one large adult handful):

- 1 cup baking soda
- ¾ cup water
- ½ cup cornstarch
- Food colouring
- ½ tablespoon vegetable glycerin (optional)

Method:

1. Mix baking soda and cornstarch in a saucepan.
2. Add the water.
3. Put on the stove on medium heat.
4. Stir the mixture. It will be watery at first but the cornstarch will cause it to thicken fairly quickly.

5. Add a few drops of your chosen food colouring to the mixture now or, if you're making an extra large batch and want to split it up into different colours, wait until after step 7.
6. Stir until the mixture starts to clump around the spoon. This should take less than five minutes.
7. Remove the saucepan from the heat.
8. Add the vegetable glycerin if you are using it. It will make the playdough less drying on little hands.
9. Keep stirring. The playdough will get smoother and more solid.
10. Transfer your new soft, smooth, allergen-free playdough onto a smooth surface to cool.
11. Play! Build towers, use cookie cutters of different sizes and shapes, use a toy rolling pin... Get creative!

Tips:

- Store the playdough in an airtight container in the fridge. It will last for around 4-5 uses with grubby toddler fingers.

- Get your Montessori hat on and store the plastic cookie cutters and toy rolling pin together in a low drawer where your child can get them by herself.

- Mix in some glitter as well when you're adding food colouring for a special treat.

- Tell all your friends about gluten-free playdough and make it a 'normal' thing so that children with wheat allergy and coeliac disease don't have to be excluded.

* Disclaimer: The hours of fun are not consecutive, they are a sum total. No toddler can sit still, engaged in one quiet activity, for more than 30 minutes. And that's on a good day when all your stars have aligned. But if you are an exhausted parent like me, you'll take what you can get!

Chapter 19
Wheat Substitutes

More and more people are choosing to go gluten free. Whatever the reason behind this switch - wheat allergy, gluten hypersensitivity or dietary fad - the mass demand means more options and lower costs for everyone.

Below are the most common alternatives to wheat-based foods. Your choice will depend on several factors like other allergies, health factors, and taste. The cost of each option will vary depending on geographic location and retailer.

Gluten-Free Ready Foods

The quickest, but potentially most expensive, option is to switch to gluten-free alternatives to all your everyday foods. Many supermarkets now carry several brands of gluten-free bread, pasta, cakes and cookies. Some of these are very good substitutes for wheat products and taste virtually the same. Schar, which is headquartered in Germany but has products all over the world, has the lead in both quality and variety. Their baked goods - breads, cakes and biscuits - taste just like the real deal but are pricier than I would prefer. Although the company has had a head start (they've been at this for over 30 years), other manufacturers are catching up fast. In fact some supermarkets are now offering their own brand of gluten-free alternatives that taste great and are more budget-friendly.

If you are avoiding wheat but not gluten, you can consume foods made with rye and barley. Traditional Eastern European rye breads can be easier to source and more cost-effective than specialty gluten-free loaves. Oats, as long as they are labelled gluten-free, are also a great option.

Flour Substitutes

Gluten-free flour mixes are now available in many supermarkets and easy to order online. They often contain a mix of other grains like rice, amaranth and quinoa, and sometimes even potato flour. They can be used as a straight (1:1) substitute for wheat flour in recipes. However, as other grains lack the stickiness of gluten, you may need to add xanthan gum to your recipe (at a ratio of ¼ teaspoon per cup of gluten-free flour) to get the same texture as wheat-based baked goods. Check the ingredients list before doing this as some gluten-free baking mixes already contain it.

As long as you are not allergic to it, almond flour can be a great option if you are avoiding wheat. Nuts are packed with plant-based protein, vitamins and minerals so making this switch could take the guilt out of your morning muffin (as long as you reduce the added sugar). Gluten-free cakes in trendier cafes are often made with almond flour.

Pizza

Apart from store-bought gluten-free options, there are three homemade versions that have received the approval of my family and friends.

- Flat breads like Mexican tortillas made from corn and rice are perfect ready-made pizza bases. They are an extremely easy swap and if you have fussy eaters, they are a great option for getting children involved in cooking and excited about eating. Kids can add their own toppings in different patterns and won't have to wait long for the 'pizza' to bake.
- Tofu (yes, tofu!) can make a great pizza base, as long as you are not allergic to soy. Granted it won't be in the circular shape we all know and love but it will be gluten-free, low-carb, keto-friendly and vegan, making you very trendy

indeed. Use firm tofu, sliced into 1-2cm rectangles, and top them with all your favourites.

- Cauliflower pizza base has gained much popularity with the rise of the ketogenic movement making them so mainstream that you can often find them in the frozen food aisle of large supermarkets. If you'd like more control over ingredients (the ready made ones usually contain eggs) and you're up for a slightly messy challenge, there are plenty of recipes on how to do it yourself online.

Varying the Menu

Another option is to substitute the actual foods on your family's menu. The options are endless. Instead of sandwiches, you could have wraps with gluten-free tortilla bread. Rice and potatoes alone are incredibly versatile and can be boiled, baked, fried and much more. Asian cuisines are more rice-based so may be worth exploring. A great substitute for soya sauce, which contains wheat, is its gluten-free cousin 'tamari'.

You may find that removing pasta and bread from the table ends up being a blessing. For my family it forced us to eat more vegetables and my children genuinely enjoy them now. Root vegetables like carrots and yams add satisfying starch to a meal while boosting the nutritional content. Other vegetables are a bonus. Cauliflower, broccoli, mushrooms, spinach, aubergines... You are only limited by your imagination.

:: Helpful Hint: Eating Out with Allergies

Although you have the most control over what is in your food if you cook it yourself, having allergies does not mean that you can never eat at a restaurant. There are restaurants and cafes that cater specifically to those with food allergies in some large cities. These are particularly useful if you are avoiding multiple food groups and some of them are outstanding. Have a look online to see if there are any in your area. If not, below are some tips for when you want to venture out to a 'regular' eatery:

- Always have two epinephrine auto-injectors with you.
- Don't dine alone.
- Make sure your fellow diners know what to look out for in an allergic reaction and what they must do in an emergency.
- Know the location and route to the nearest hospital. The closer it is, the better.
- Some cuisines naturally contain less wheat than others making them more amenable for those with wheat allergy. For example, Indian, Ethiopian, Mexican and Colombian cuisines tend to contain less wheat. Cuisines like Japanese, Korean, and Chinese can be an option if you avoid ready-made sauces like soy sauce, hoisin sauce etc.
- Large international chains tend to have allergy policies and consistency in their recipes, making them a safer bet than independent mom-and-pop shops.
- Buffets pose an additional risk of cross-contamination so avoid these. Even dishes that are not made with your allergen(s) can have traces in them from other patrons mixing up serving spoons.
- Make sure you can communicate clearly in the same language as the restaurant staff.

- Explain that you have severe allergies and would like to speak to a manager. They may have recommendations on items on the menu that must be avoided.
- Enquire about the ingredients in every item you are thinking of ordering, running through the checklist of "wheat, bread, flour, soy sauce..."' with the staff to make sure these are not in your food.
- Wipe down all surfaces - tables and chairs - with soap and water in case of trace amounts left by the last diner. With all the extra cleaning done due to CoVID-19, people will not think you are a nut (no pun intended).
- Once your food has arrived, check with the staff again that it does not contain your allergens.

Chapter 20
Daycare, School and Work

Wheat allergy can be particularly challenging for very young children at daycare or school as most conventional everyday foods contain it. Daycares are not able to eliminate wheat which means allergy parents often live in fear of crumbs at snack time or, worse yet, food getting mixed up.

Once children are a bit older, the difficulty is more that they don't want to stand out as different from their peers so they may engage in risky behaviour such as not asking if something contains wheat, or not carrying their epinephrine auto-injector. Refer back to Part 2 on practices to help raise confident, empowered kids for more on this topic.

Gluten-free alternatives, though more easily accessible nowadays, are not always available when you need them. Moreover, they can be expensive. This can make it hard to convince some establishments to offer them.

Here are some tips to help the transition to a new 'allergy-safe' reality outside the home.

- **Be clear:** Ask your school or workplace how they manage people with allergies. Do they have smaller classes, clean tables more frequently, have designated food-consumption spots, or maybe even exclude allergens completely? Find a compromise that makes you feel safe yet is not so restrictive for everyone to make you a pariah.

- **Don't let cost be an excuse:** As gluten-free options can be more expensive, some schools and workplaces can be hesitant to add them. Offer to provide your own if needed and be clear that it must be kept separate from wheat products to avoid confusion. You may find, as I often did, that the establishment realises their inhumanity and offers to stock a wheat-free option for you.

- **Do your part:** Think of ways to avoid resistance. Find alternatives for food, recipes etc to save the institution time and effort. If money seems to be a sticking point, consider subsidising the cost. It may not be fair, but it is safe.

- **Teach your teachers:** If the wheat-allergic person is your child, ask to have a short meeting with the staff where you can discuss your child's allergens. Bring along the Anaphylaxis Action Plan given to you by your doctor and discuss what teachers should look out for, including any behaviours particular to your child.

- **Food for thought:** Ask to change to non-food treats for celebrations. In addition to being more allergy-friendly, taking the emphasis away from food helps fight the obesity epidemic. There is no reason that occasions need to be celebrated with pizza and cakes. Games, gifts, spa treatments etc can be more fun. Halloween and Valentines Day could be celebrated with bat- or heart-shaped stationery instead of candy.

Chapter 21
Travelling with Food Allergies

Going on vacation with allergies can be stressful. Even after you have informed the airline and the hotel of any allergies, you still need to remain vigilant and often have to source some of your own food anyway.

We first discovered our daughter's allergies while on holiday. We attempted one more beach holiday two years later in the Bahamas. It was a disaster. She was starving for most of the week and then ended up having a reaction anyway after playing with the bowl of sugar sachets on the table! Our stress levels were so high that only as I was packing to leave did I realise that a purse with some cash and my wedding ring had been stolen from the safe! After this, we decided to change our strategy as an allergy family.

Here are some tips for vacationing with food allergies:

- Consider only visiting places you know very well yourself or have deep relationships you can rely on. For us this was London, England, where my husband and I used to live. As locals, we knew where to source everything we might need as well as all the local hospitals and pharmacies.

- Take spare medication - both epinephrine auto-injectors and antihistamines. While you might normally carry two EpiPens, when travelling abroad consider taking four if you can.

- Invest in health insurance. For our trip to the Dominican Republic where we first experienced the horror of anaphylaxis, I insisted on getting insurance for every member of the family. My husband thought the $190 was a waste of money until it meant we were refunded the full $1400 we paid for our daughter's medical treatment.

- Take some non-perishable foods with you that you know you/your child enjoys in case the allergy-friendly options are not to your taste.

- Realise that your diet will not be optimal. We accepted that even with our best efforts, jumping through hoops and bending over backwards as we always did for our child, she would end up losing some weight during our visit abroad but would have a tremendous amount of fun.

- Wipe down all dining surfaces for kids - table, chairs, condiment containers etc - with soap and water. Children tend to touch every single surface and always seem to put their hands in their eyes, nose or mouth.

- Try to be flexible. You may end up eating the same foods over and over again. Or you may end up eating things you normally consider 'unhealthy'. Remember, the important thing is just to eat. Everything will go back to normal once you are home.

- Consider getting 'allergy translation cards' where common phrases related to your allergen are detailed in the language of your choice. I have not used these as our strategy for now is to only vacation in countries we know well ourselves or have excellent contacts, but I imagine these cards can be useful. Moreover, knowing how to communicate your allergies in as many ways as possible can only be a good thing.

PART 4
LOOKING TO THE FUTURE

Food allergies are a complex and fascinating field, with a great deal of research going on around the world. Most of the work focuses on the following broad areas:

- Risk factors for becoming allergic
- Diagnosis of allergies and predicting severity
- Treatment
- Improving quality of life

It is impossible to cover all the current research in just one chapter (or indeed one book!). This section will highlight a few developments that might change how we manage allergies in the near future.

Finding the right answers to the puzzle requires a multidisciplinary approach involving immunologists, gastroenterologists and bioengineering. But first we need the right questions.

Why do some people develop allergies?

Some of the risk factors that lead to a person developing allergies have already been uncovered. For example, the dual allergen exposure hypothesis showed that having uncontrolled eczema with extensive patches where the skin barrier is damaged can lead to sensitisation to a food protein and potentially food allergies.

More clues are now emerging from data logged as part of the CHILD study in Canada. Researchers collected data from over 3400 children, following them from the third trimester in the womb to age five. They looked at diet (maternal and child), birth and breastfeeding information, stool, urine and blood analysis, sleep patterns, geographical location, living conditions as well as a range of other factors. Scientists are now wading through this huge bank of information to find correlations such as:

- A baby's first poo can predict food allergies, i.e. the more diverse the molecules and microorganisms in a baby's first stool (meconium) the less likely they are to develop allergies in future.
- Exposure to air pollution while in the womb and infancy increase the risk of allergy.
- Eczema in infancy does not predict the development of asthma. Once a child with eczema becomes sensitised to food proteins, they are seven times more likely to continue the atopic march and develop asthma and, later, food allergies.

South of the border, in the United States, a group from the Broad Institute at the Massachusetts Institute of Technology is using CRISPR, a gene-editing tool that has revolutionised the field, to look at which genes are involved in allergic reactions and what role they play once it has begun. The team is also investigating how the gut microbiome is involved.

Why do some people become sensitised but not allergic?

Not everyone who is sensitised to a certain food protein will go on to develop an allergy. In fact, research into peanut allergy by different groups found completely different numbers ranging from 11% to 65% of sensitised people becoming allergic.

The key to why some people become sensitised but never have an allergic reaction is considered the 'holy grail' of allergy research. Everything else - including diagnosis and treatment - follows from this.

Until recently, much of the focus when discussing allergic diseases has been on the antibody immunoglobulin E (IgE) and mast cells but other key players have begun to emerge. Basophils, another type of white blood cell similar to mast cells, have been shown to have a starring role in both IgE-mediated allergic reactions and other inflammatory conditions including asthma and eosinophilic oesophagitis.

Once activated, basophils release chemicals that drive the allergic response. In fact, the basophil activation test (BAT) has been shown to be able to differentiate between those who are sensitised but not allergic to peanuts, and those who will have an allergic reaction if exposed to the legume (remember, peanuts are legumes and not nuts). The team, led by Dr Alexandra Santos, is based at King's College London, just like the researchers who came up with ground-breaking findings like LEAP and the Dual-Allergen Exposure Hypothesis discussed in Chapter 7. The test is already being used on an experimental basis at some large research hospitals around the world.

Why do some people who were once allergic outgrow allergies naturally?

This question points to the plasticity of the immune system, especially in early life, and shows that if the right markers are targeted, we could treat allergies and perhaps even 'cure' them.

If DNA can be thought of as a recipe for how the body should do something, then DNA methylation, a tag that attaches itself to the DNA, is an additional note that changes how the body reads the instructions. This is the idea behind the work at the Max-Delbruck Centre for Molecular Medicine in Berlin, Germany. The team is screening the entire genome (the 'cookbook' that has all the instructions that govern our bodily processes) to see which genes need their recipes changed in order to retrain the body to tolerate allergens. They are also looking at genetic markers that might indicate when tolerance is reached during OIT so that patients know when they can stop immunotherapy.

Another group in Australia is investigating whether we can use stem cells to make the body effectively forget it was allergic. The team, led by Dr Jane AlKouba at the University of Queensland, extracted stem cells from the bone marrow of mice and added an extra gene. Then, they injected the modified stem cells back into the mice and induced an allergic response to hen's egg. The new blood cells that were produced went on to switch off the allergic response by effectively silencing the responses from immune cells called T-helper 2 cells.

In addition to combing through the genes behind allergies, the Food Allergy Science Initiative team at the Broad Institute has identified both a type of cell and a chemical messenger that magnify allergic reactions. When allergens enter the gut, the neuropeptide (chemical messenger) Neuromedin U amplifies the response driven by cells called innate lymphoid cells. These cells are now emerging as critical to allergy development. The team is now working on altering that communication before the allergic reaction starts.

There are other chemicals that are now well-known to act as messengers in an allergic reaction, signalling processes to begin. Interleukins are a type of chemical messenger that are secreted by cells in the immune system, like basophils described earlier, when they are activated. Interleukin 4 (IL-4) and Interleukin-13 (IL-13) are the main proteins that signal the production of IgE. The use of biologic agents, called 'monoclonal antibodies', to block these messengers has proved effective in treating other inflammatory conditions.

Recent research at McMaster University in Canada used one of these antibodies, *dupilumab*, in conjunction with oral immunotherapy in mice. The results were so compelling that they may point to a potential cure for food allergies. Different biologic agents have been developed to work on different molecules of the immune response. They tend to have names that end in '-mab', like *dupilumab, omalizumab* or *etokimab*. Dr Manel Jordana, one of the leads of this study, feels this approach of using a biologic agent alongside oral immunotherapy could be the most effective way to train the body to not react to allergens. Using driving a car as an analogy, he described the process as 'stepping on the gas' with OIT and then 'turning the steering wheel' by deviating the immune response using the biologic agent.

How can we improve the quality of life of allergic individuals?

Although effective strides have been made in looking for a viable treatment or cure for food allergies, finding it may take a while. In the meantime, researchers and private companies are working on ways to make life a bit easier for those with allergies.

- Some research is going into identifying the problematic proteins in common foods that cause allergies, e.g. peanuts, and then removing them to make an allergen-free alternative. Although this might solve the problem of feeling left out when others are eating a certain food, it is effectively like finding another food substitution, akin to using rice milk instead of cow's milk. It does not lessen the risk of a reaction from accidental exposure to the regular protein. In fact, it may cause more confusion and increase that risk.
- Realising that epinephrine auto-injectors (EAIs) are often underused due to cost and fear, pharmaceutical firms are developing epinephrine nasal sprays that can be used instead.
- Wearable devices that detect a histamine spike, and thereby an allergic reaction, are being developed. These alert the user, their caregivers and perhaps even emergency services when an allergic reaction is detected, as well as showing the location of the person and their nearest EAI.
- Devices to detect the presence of allergens in foods are also in the works. There are several products being developed, each using different technologies. Although they offer some hope, it is worth noting that such gadgets do not need approval from safety governing bodies like the FDA so will

not undergo the level of rigorous testing that you might want for something as serious as food allergies.

Although the above research areas are diverse, they are just the tip of the iceberg. Peanut allergy is still the most studied food allergy as it causes the largest number of fatalities and, unlike egg or dairy, does not tend to be outgrown. For a landmark study like LEAP, which showed that early introduction can prevent allergies, it was chosen for three reasons:

- The reaction is usually seen the first or second time a peanut is eaten.
- There was 'control' data available from Israel.
- There was funding.

This highlights the key bottlenecks in finding further answers for food allergies, especially to other allergens – access to enough data and funding.

Nonetheless, the technologies described in this section, though still unproven, do provide hope. In addition to increased awareness by those with allergies as well as those without, the rise in the number of allergen-free food alternatives and treatments that already work is making the world safer and easier for those with food allergies. The discoveries on the horizon will just make things better.

FURTHER READING
THE IMMUNE SYSTEM AND
ALLERGY

With all the talk of IgE, it would be remiss not to look into this antibody as well as what happens in the body during an allergic reaction. This section will explore the main antibodies, chemicals and cells involved in allergies.

If Latin words and acronyms make you yawn, feel free to skip this section. You can always refer back here if you are intrigued later. On the other hand, if you find the workings of the human body fascinating, as I do, read on for some amazing biology.

The immune system is the body's natural defense system. It is very complex. Unlike many other bodily systems, the organs of the immune system are not arranged linearly, physically touching each other. They are located in different parts of the body and all make white blood cells and antibodies of different kinds. These cells and antibodies are the body's frontline fighters against diseases and infections.

Gamed by Little Goblins

Immunoglobulins are Y-shaped antibodies. They are made in the blood and lymph nodes by a type of white blood cell called plasma cells. Around 20,000 immunoglobulins are produced per second. There are five different types - G, A, M, E, D - with different structures and functions.

Immunoglobulin G (IgG): This is the smallest but most common antibody. Making up about 75%-80% of the antibodies in the body, it is found in all body fluids, including blood. IgG protects against bacterial and viral infections but can take time to form after an infection or immunisation. IgG is the only type of antibody that can cross the placenta in a pregnant woman to protect the unborn baby. Special subclasses (types) of this antibody are now thought to be involved in allergies.

Immunoglobulin A (IgA): This antibody is found in the linings of the respiratory tract and digestive system, as well as in saliva (spit), tears, and breast milk. IgA protects the surfaces of the body that are exposed to the outside.

Immunoglobulin M (IgM): Found mainly in blood and lymph fluid, this is the first antibody the body makes when it fights a new infection. IgM is the biggest antibody. It can direct other cells in the immune system to destroy foreign substances.

Immunoglobulin E (IgE): This antibody defends against parasites, venoms and toxins. Everybody normally has small amounts of IgE in the blood but the levels are higher when the body is fighting an infection and in allergic individuals. IgE is also found in lungs, skin and mucous membranes. It is the primary molecule that drives immediate allergic reactions and therefore what allergy tests try to detect. It lives approximately 3 weeks. If it binds to many parts of the mast cell, the reaction will be more severe

Immunoglobulin D (IgD): This is the least understood antibody, with only trace amounts in the blood.

Mast-ive Attack

In addition to IgE antibodies, special cells called *mast cells* play a starring role in allergic reactions. Mast cells originate in the bone marrow and travel to locations around the body where they fully mature. They are concentrated in the lining of the skin, nose, eyes, lungs, gut and blood vessels. When there is an allergic reaction, these locations are where symptoms are typically seen. Mast cells contain *granules* of chemicals like histamine, heparin and serotonin.

Research is now uncovering that there may be three other key players in IgE-mediated allergic reactions:

- Basophils
- IgG1
- IgG4

Basophils are a type of white blood cell that circulate around the body. They are made in the bone marrow. Like mast cells, they contain granules of chemicals and are activated by IgE antibodies that are formed in response to an allergen. Meanwhile, IgG1 and IgG4 are special types of IgG antibodies described earlier. It is thought that IgG1 might be involved when a person first develops food allergies and in keeping them allergic. On the other hand, IgG4 seems to have a role when allergies resolve. The function and mechanism of basophils, IgG1, IgG4, as well as other molecules and cells are still being studied.

Locked and Loaded

The first time an allergy-prone person encounters the allergen, the body, thinking it is a threat, might make a large amount of IgE antibodies specific to that allergen. The person would then be 'sensitised' to that allergen. This *allergen specific IgE* (sIgE) can be measured in blood tests. These antibodies then attach to mast cells around the body. The next time the allergen enters the body, the receptors on these IgE antibodies recognise it and, like dominoes dropping, the body sets off a cascade of procedures in an effort to protect itself.

The mast cells open up to release their contents. This is called 'degranulation'. Chemicals like histamine cause blood vessels to widen and become leakier causing low blood pressure, and other tissues to swell including in the airways, making it harder to breathe. Muscles in the digestive tract tighten, causing cramps, diarrhoea and/or vomiting. Histamine acts on the nerves causing itchiness. All the symptoms are the body's attempt to expel what it thinks is an invader.

ACKNOWLEDGEMENTS

Just as it takes a village to raise a child, it takes a population to finish a project. This book would still be a collection of jumbled thoughts in my head without the guidance, encouragement and belief of some very special people.

Without the hard-work, dedication and, frankly, genius of the doctors and research scientists on whose work this book is based, we would be nowhere. From myself, my family and the global allergy community, THANK YOU.

Many thanks also to all the doctors, nurses, dieticians, phlebotomists, and allergy families who were gracious enough to speak to me.

I'd like to thank Dr Rhoda Kagan in particular. Her contribution to this journey has been massive. Not only a brilliant allergist but a highly-adept and compassionate paediatrician, Dr Kagan went above and beyond allergies, making sure every aspect of my child's health was progressing. Without her my child would not be the healthy, precocious being that we see today. She helped us through the most difficult years of our lives, all the while answering my many, many questions about food allergies. My family will forever be indebted to her, as well as Debbie and Rachel in her office.

I am grateful to Dr Julia Upton, from The Hospital for Sick Kids in Totonto, for taking the time, even at 9pm on a chilly Canadian Tuesday evening, to advise and encourage me to contribute to the allergy community and forge my own path.

I owe much to my teacher and mentor Prof Lis Howell of City University London. On top of proof-reading the first draft of this book and offering valuable insights, it was she who instilled in me how to be a *journalist* - to hunt down answers and then communicate them clearly and effectively. More than a decade later, her wisdom and guidance still serve me well.

I'd like to thank Giselle Brown from GDB Legal for her advice, warmth and continued friendship.

To Helene Enahoro, Rebecca Nam and Ven Paldano, I owe my life. For over 25 years they have been the best friends in the world, especially my 'twinnie'. I am so lucky.

My utmost gratitude goes to my mum, Firoza, who made me who I am today. I miss her all day every day but know we will be reunited someday. Until then, I continue to work hard to make her proud.

A big thank you to my husband Jeremy for all his support for this and every other crazy project.

And last but definitely *most*, I'd like to thank my two kids, especially SA who has been my guinea pig and my hero. Every single day, I thank God for giving me these little girls. They fill my life with joy and are braver and stronger than anyone I know. They are my inspiration.

HELPFUL RESOURCES

Print-Outs and Additional Information

Allergy Guides.com
https://allergy-guides.com

Information and Support Groups

Food Allergy Research & Education (FARE)
https://www.foodallergy.org/

Allergy UK
https://www.allergyuk.org/

Food Allergy Canada
https://foodallergycanada.ca/

Coeliac UK
https://www.coeliac.org.uk

Cooking with Allergies

Kids With Food Allergies
https://www.kidswithfoodallergies.org/

Allergy Translation Cards

Anaphylaxis Campaign
https://www.anaphylaxis.org.uk/living-with-anaphylaxis/travelling/translation-cards/

REFERENCES

PART 1

1. "Non-IgE Mediated Food Allergy", Royal Children's Hospital Melbourne https://www.rch.org.au/uploadedFiles/Main/Content/allergy/Non%20IgE%20Food%20Allergy.pdf
2. Dr Philippe Begin, "Understand the severity of your food allergy", Webinar, Food Allergy Canada. 28 September 2021
3. "Pollen Food Syndrome", Anaphylaxis Campaign, July 2019. https://www.anaphylaxis.org.uk/wp-content/uploads/2019/07/Pollen-food-2017.pd
4. Milton Gold, *The Complete Kid's Allergy and Asthma Guide: The Parent's Handbook for Children of All Ages* (Robert Rose Inc, 2003)
5. "Food Protein-Induced Allergic Proctocolitis (FPIAP)", Australasian Society of Clinical Immunology and Allergy https://www.allergy.org.au/patients/food-other-adverse-reactions/proctocolitis-fpiap
6. "Food Protein-Induced Enterocolitis Syndrome (FPIES)", Australasian Society of Clinical Immunology and Allergy https://www.allergy.org.au/patients/food-other-adverse-reactions/food-protein-induced-enterocolitis-syndrome-fpies
7. "Eosinophilic Oesophagitis (EoE)", Australasian Society of Clinical Immunology and Allergy, https://www.allergy.org.au/patients/food-other-adverse-reactions/eosinophilic-oesophagitis
8. Keet CA, Matsui EC, Dhillon G, Lenehan P, Paterakis M, Wood RA. The natural history of wheat allergy. Ann Allergy Asthma Immunol. 2009 May;102(5):410-5. doi:

10.1016/S1081-1206(10)60513-3. PMID: 19492663. https://pubmed.ncbi.nlm.nih.gov/19492663/
9. "Wheat: quality and characteristic requirements", S. Uthayakumaran and C.W. Wrigley, *Cereal Grains*, (Woodhead Publishing Ltd, 2010)
10. "Connecting the Dots between Allergies and Autoimmune Disease", Benaroya Research Institute, 31 July 2017 https://www.benaroyaresearch.org/blog/post/connectin g-dots-between-allergies-and-autoimmune-disease
11. "About coeliac disease", Coeliac UK https://www.coeliac.org.uk/information-and-support/coeliac-disease/about-coeliac-disease/
12. Lee Falin PhD, "What is Gluten?", Quick & Dirty Tips https://www.quickanddirtytips.com/education/science/ what-is-gluten
13. Roxanne Khamsi, ""Gluten Sensitivity" May be a Misnomer for Distinct Illnesses to Various Wheat Proteins", Scientific American, 1 February 2014 https://www.scientificamerican.com/article/gluten-sensitivity-may-be-a-misnomer-for-distinct-illnesses-to-various-wheat-proteins/
14. Dr Cynthia Popalis, paediatric gastroenterologist, Boomerang Health/Toronto Sick Kids, conversations with the author 2016-2018
15. Sense About Science - Making Sense of Allergies https://senseaboutscience.org/wp-content/uploads/2016/09/Making-Sense-of-Allergies-1.pdf
16. Colic - Stanford Children's Health https://www.stanfordchildrens.org/en/topic/default?id =colic-90-P01985
17. Venter, C., Pereira, B., Voigt, K., Grundy, J., Clayton, C.B., Higgins, B., Arshad, S.H. and Dean, T. (2008), Original article: Prevalence and cumulative incidence of food hypersensitivity in the first 3 years of life. Allergy, 63: 354-359. https://doi.org/10.1111/j.1398-9995.2007.01570.x
18. Jacobson D, Mireskandari K, Cohen E. An 11-Year-Old Boy With Vision Loss. JAMA Pediatr. 2017;171(12):1226–1227.

doi:10.1001/jamapediatrics.2017.2543
https://jamanetwork.com/journals/jamapediatrics/articl
e-abstract/2654882

19. "Food Allergies | FDA", US Food and Drug Administration
https://www.fda.gov/food/food-labeling-
nutrition/food-allergies

20. "Common Food Allergens", Government of Canada
https://www.canada.ca/en/health-
canada/services/food-nutrition/food-safety/food-
allergies-intolerances/food-allergies.html

21. "14 Allergens", Food Standards Agency,
https://www.food.gov.uk/sites/default/files/media/doc
ument/top-allergy-types.pdf

22. "List of 14 Allergens", Food Safety Authority of Ireland
https://www.fsai.ie/legislation/food_legislation/food_in
formation/14_allergens.html

23. "10 Most Common Food Allergies in Australia", Australian
Institute of Food Safety,
https://www.foodsafety.com.au/blog/top-10-most-
common-food-allergies

24. "Non-Food Allergens", Food Allergy Research and
Education, https://www.foodallergy.org/resources/non-
food-allergens

25. "Latex Allergy", Better Health Channel,
https://www.betterhealth.vic.gov.au/health/conditionsa
ndtreatments/latex-allergy

26. Ravn NH, Halling AS, Berkowitz AG, Rinnov MR,
Silverberg JI, Egeberg A et al. How does parental history of
atopic disease predict the risk of atopic dermatitis in a child?
A systematic review and meta-analysis. J Allergy Clin
Immunol. 2020 Apr;145(4):1182-1193. doi:
10.1016/j.jaci.2019.12.899.
https://www.jacionline.org/article/S0091-6749(19)32606-
5/fulltext

27. Hill DA and Spergel JM. The Atopic March: Critical
Evidence and Clinical Relevance, Ann Allergy Asthma
Immunol. 2018 Feb; 120(2): 131–137

https://www.annallergy.org/article/S1081-1206(17)31258-9/fulltext
28. "Interview with George Du Toit on Pediatric Allergy", EAACI European Academy of Allergy and CLinical Immunology, YouTube, June 25 , 2019 https://www.youtube.com/watch?v=e_sDQc4un60
29. Flohr C, Perkin M, Logan K, Marrs T, Radulovic S, Campbell LE, MacCallum SF, McLean WHI, Lack G. Atopic dermatitis and disease severity are the main risk factors for food sensitization in exclusively breastfed infants. J Invest Dermatol. 2014 Feb;134(2):345-350 https://pubmed.ncbi.nlm.nih.gov/23867897/
30. Lack G, Fox D, Northstone K, Golding J. Avon Longitudinal Study of Parents and Children Study Team. Factors associated with the development of peanut allergy in childhood. N Engl J Med 2003;348:977-85. https://www.nejm.org/doi/full/10.1056/nejmoa013536
31. Fox AT, Sasieni P, du Toit G, Syed H, Lack G. Household peanut consumption as a risk factor for the development of peanut allergy. J Allergy Clin Immunol 2009; 123:417-23. https://www.jacionline.org/article/S0091-6749(08)02431-7/fulltext
32. Lack G. Epidemiologic risks for food allergy. J Allergy Clin Immunol 2008;121: 1331-6. https://www.jacionline.org/article/S0091-6749(08)00778-1/fulltext
33. Prof Gideon Lack, "How Does Food Allergy Develop?", Presentation.
34. Du Toit G, Katz Y, Sasieni P, Mesher D, Maleki SJ, Fisher HR, et al. Early consumption of peanuts in infancy is associated with a low prevalence of peanut allergy. J Allergy Clin Immunol 2008; 122:984-91. https://www.jacionline.org/article/S0091-6749(08)01698-9/fulltext
35. Rudders SA, Camargo CA Jr. Sunlight, vitamin D and food allergy. Curr Opin Allergy Clin Immunol. 2015 Aug;15(4):350-7. https://pubmed.ncbi.nlm.nih.gov/26110686/

36. The Maternal Infant Microbiome: Considerations for Labour and Birth https://www.ncbi.nlm.nih.gov/pmc/articles/PMC564860 5/

PART 2

37. Dr Kathy Weston, "How to Raise a Resilient Child", Webinar, 26 May 2021
38. "Tools for Managing Stress and Anxiety | Huberman Lab Podcast #10", 8 March 2021 https://youtu.be/ntfcfJ28eiU
39. Sheryl Sandberg and Adam Grant, *Option B: Facing Adversity, Building Resilience, and Finding Joy* (WH Allen, 2017)
40. Alvord, M. K., & Grados, J. J. (2005). Enhancing Resilience in Children: A Proactive Approach. *Professional Psychology: Research and Practice*, 36(3), 238–245. https://doi.org/10.1037/0735-7028.36.3.238

PART 3

41. Dr Helen Brough, Allergy Academy: 11th food allergy study day, Royal Society of Medicine, 25 May 2017
42. Dr Robert Boyle, Allergy Academy: 11th food allergy study day, Royal Society of Medicine, 25 May 2017
43. "Advancing the management of cow's milk protein allergy - Anna Nowak-Wegrzyn" - Nestle Nutrition Institute, YouTube, 10 June 2021 https://www.youtube.com/watch?v=vTpSyRxy-oo
44. Ayechu-Muruzabal V, van Stigt AH, Mank M, Willemsen LEM, Stahl B et al. Diversity of Human Milk Oligosaccharides and Effects on Early Life Immune Development. Front. Pediatr. 2018 September. https://doi.org/10.3389/fped.2018.0023
45. Evelina Children's Hospital GSTT allergy specialist dieticians, conversation with the author, 16 December 2020

46. Kusunoki T, Mukaida K, Morimoto T, Sakuma M, Yasumi T, Nishikomori R, Heike T. Birth order effect on childhood food allergy. Pediatr Allergy Immunol. 2012 May;23(3):250-4. https://doi.org/10.1111/j.1399-3038.2011.01246.x

47. Munblit D, Perkin MR, Palmer DJ, Allen KJ, Boyle RJ. Assessment of Evidence About Common Infant Symptoms and Cow's Milk Allergy. JAMA Pediatr. 2020;174(6):599–608. https://jamanetwork.com/journals/jamapediatrics/article-abstract/2764081

48. Prof George Du Toit, Allergy Academy: 11th food allergy study day, Royal Society of Medicine, 25 May 2017

49. "Food allergy in under 19s: assessment and diagnosis", National Institute for Health and Care Excellence, 23 February 2011 https://www.nice.org.uk/guidance/cg116/chapter/1-Guidance#alternative-diagnostic-tools

50. Wang J, Jones SM, Pongracic JA, Song Y, Yang N, Sicherer SH et al. Safety, clinical, and immunologic efficacy of a Chinese herbal medicine (Food Allergy Herbal Formula-2) for food allergy. J Allergy Clin Immunol. 2015 Oct;136(4):962-970.e1. https://pubmed.ncbi.nlm.nih.gov/26044855/

51. Shen Shen Tang Herbs, Richmond Hill, conversations with the author, 2015-2016

52. Dr Julia Upton, Toronto Anaphylaxis Education Group meeting, 17 April 2018

53. Dr Rhoda Kagan, conversations with the author, 2015 - 2019

54. "Cross-Reactivity - A Definition", Anaphylaxis Campaign, March 2019 https://www.anaphylaxis.org.uk/knowledgebase/cross-reactivity

55. Toronto Sick Kids Hospital phlebotomists, conversations with the author, 2016

56. "Ask the Expert | ImmunoCap sIgE", American Academy of Asthma Allergy & Immunology, 1 November 2017

https://www.aaaai.org/allergist-resources/ask-the-expert/answers/old-ask-the-experts/immunocap-sige

57. Cianferoni, A., Khullar, K., Saltzman, R. et al. Oral food challenge to wheat: a near-fatal anaphylaxis and review of 93 food challenges in children. World Allergy Organ J 6, 1–10 (2013). https://doi.org/10.1186/1939-4551-6-14

58. Perry TT, Matsui EC, Conover-Walker MK, Wood RA: Risk of oral food challenges. J Allergy Clin Immunol. 2004, 114: 1164-1168. 10.1016/j.jaci.2004.07.063. https://www.jacionline.org/article/S0091-6749(04)02289-4/fulltext

59. Fleischer DM, Bock A, Spears GC, Wilson CG, Miyazawa NK, Gleason MC et al. Oral Food Challenges in Children with a Diagnosis Of Food Allergy. J Peds 2011;158(4):578-583. https://www.jpeds.com/article/S0022-3476(10)00787-0/fulltext

60. Dr Paul Turner, Allergy Academy: 11th food allergy study day, Royal Society of Medicine, 25 May 2017

61. "Alabama Boy, 3, Dies of Severe Reaction During Baked Milk Challenge". Allergic Living, 2 August 2017. https://www.allergicliving.com/2017/08/02/alabama-boy-3-dies-of-severe-reaction-during-baked-milk-challenge-test/

62. Leeds S, Liu EG, Nowak-Wegrzyn A. Wheat oral immunotherapy. Curr Opin Allergy Clin Immunol. 2021 Jun 1;21(3):269-277. doi: 10.1097/ACI.0000000000000743. PMID: 33840798. https://pubmed.ncbi.nlm.nih.gov/33840798/

63. Nowak-Węgrzyn A, Wood RA, Nadeau KC, Pongracic JA, Henning AK, Lindblad RW, Beyer K, Sampson HA. Multicenter, randomized, double-blind, placebo-controlled clinical trial of vital wheat gluten oral immunotherapy. J Allergy Clin Immunol. 2019 Feb;143(2):651-661.e9. doi: 10.1016/j.jaci.2018.08.041. https://pubmed.ncbi.nlm.nih.gov/30389226/

64. Sato S, Utsonomiya T, Imai T, Yanagida N, Asaumi T, Ogura K et al. Wheat oral immunotherapy for wheat-induced anaphylaxis. J Allergy Clin Immunol. 2015 Oct;136(4):1131-

1133.e7 doi: 10.1016/j.jaci.2015.07.019 https://pubmed.ncbi.nlm.nih.gov/26319801/
65. Rodríguez del Río P, Díaz-Perales A, Sanchez-García S, Escudero C, do Santos P, Catarino M, Ibañez MD. Oral immunotherapy in children with IgE-mediated wheat allergy: outcome and molecular changes. J Investig Allergol Clin Immunol. 2014;24(4):240-8. PMID: 25219106. https://pubmed.ncbi.nlm.nih.gov/25219106/
66. Pacharn P, Vichyanond P. Immunotherapy for IgE-mediated wheat allergy. Hum Vaccin Immunother. 2017;13(10):2462-2466. doi:10.1080/21645515.2017.1356499 https://www.ncbi.nlm.nih.gov/pmc/articles/PMC564796 3/
67. "Ask The Expert: Wheat Desensitization Protocols", World Allergy Organization, 19 Apr 2018 https://www.worldallergy.org/ask-the-expert/questions/wheat-desensitization-protocols
68. Dr Anne Ellis, "Understanding oral allergy syndrome/pollen food syndrome", Webinar, Food Allergy Canada. 29 April 2021
69. Anagnostou K, Islam S, King Y, Foley L, Pasea L, Bond S et al. Assessing the efficacy of oral immunotherapy for the desensitisation of peanut allergy in children (STOP II): a phase 2 randomised controlled trial. Lancet. 2014 Apr 12;383(9925):1297-1304. https://www.thelancet.com/journals/lancet/article/PIIS 0140-6736(13)62301-6/fulltext
70. Wood RA. Oral Immunotherapy for Food Allergy, J Investig Allergol Clin Immunol 2017; 27(3): 151-159 doi: 10.18176/jiaci.0143. http://www.jiaci.org/revistas/vol27issue3_1.pdf
71. Baumert, J. L., Taylor, S. L. & Koppelman, S. J. Quantitative Assessment of the Safety Benefits Associated with Increasing Clinical Peanut Thresholds Through Immunotherapy. Am. Acad. Allergy, Asthma Immunol. Allergy Clin Immunol Pr. (2017). https://www.sciencedirect.com/science/article/pii/S221 3219817303677?via%3Dihub

72. Upton J, Eiwegger T. Low Dose Multi-Allergen Oral Immunotherapy for Food Allergy, 2018 Jul 4. https://clinicaltrials.gov/ProvidedDocs/28/NCT0379932 8/Prot_SAP_000.pdf

73. Kulis MD, Patil SU, Wambre E, Vickery BP. Immune mechanisms of oral immunotherapy. J Allergy Clin Immunol. 2018;141(2):491-498. https://www.ncbi.nlm.nih.gov/pmc/articles/PMC693985 8/

74. "FDA approves first drug for treatment of peanut allergy for children", 31 Jan 2020, https://www.fda.gov/news-events/press-announcements/fda-approves-first-drug-treatment-peanut-allergy-children

75. Palforzia Prescribing Information, https://www.palforzia.com/static/pi_palforzia.pdf

76. Joseph Feher, *Quantitative Human Physiology (Second Edition)*, (Academic Press, 2017)

77. "You and Your Hormones from the Society of Endocrinology", https://www.yourhormones.info/hormones/adrenaline/

78. "How to Use: Administering Your EpiPen", https://www.epipen.co.uk/en-gb/patients/your-epipen/how-to-use-your-epipen

79. Fineman SM. Optimal treatment of anaphylaxis: antihistamines versus epinephrine. Postgrad Med. 2014 Jul;126(4):73-81. https://pubmed.ncbi.nlm.nih.gov/25141245/

80. Posner LS, Camargo CA Jr. Update on the usage and safety of epinephrine auto-injectors, 2017. Drug Healthc Patient Saf. 2017;9:9-18. https://www.ncbi.nlm.nih.gov/pmc/articles/PMC536776 6/

81. Simons FE, Gu X, Simons KJ. Outdated EpiPen and EpiPen Jr autoinjectors: past their prime? J Allergy Clin Immunol. 2000 May;105(5):1025-30. https://pubmed.ncbi.nlm.nih.gov/10808186/

82. "AAAAI: Restaurant EpiPens; Devices OK After Expiration? How About After Laundering?- Roundup of epinephrine injector research prepared for AAAAI 2020", MedPage Today, 16 March 2020 https://www.medpagetoday.com/meetingcoverage/aaaa i/85441

83. Weiler JM, et al. Effects of fexofenadine, diphenhydramine, and alcohol on driving performance. A randomized, placebo-controlled trial in the Iowa driving simulator. Ann Intern Med. 2000;132(5):354–63. https://www.acpjournals.org/doi/10.7326/0003-4819-132-5-200003070-00004

84. "Blood Alcohol Content", Wikipedia. https://en.wikipedia.org/wiki/Blood_alcohol_content#L egal_limits

85. "CSACI position statement: Newer generation H1-antihistamines are safer than first-generation H1-antihistamines and should be the first-line antihistamines for the treatment of allergic rhinitis and urticaria", 1 October 2019 https://aacijournal.biomedcentral.com/articles/10.1186/s 13223-019-0375-9

86. "Tips for Giving Your Child Medication", Dana Farber Boston Childrens, 2016 http://www.danafarberbostonchildrens.org/uploadedfile s/15.%20fe_onc_tips_for_giving_medication.pdf

87. "Wheat Allergy", Food Allergy Research & Education https://www.foodallergy.org/living-food-allergies/food-allergy-essentials/common-allergens/wheat

PART 4

88. CHILD Publications, AllerGen. https://www.allergen.ca/research/scientific-publications/child-pubs/

89. Miyake K, Karasuyama H. Emerging role of basophils in allergic inflammation. Allergology International 2017; 66(3).

https://www.sciencedirect.com/science/article/pii/S132
3893017300485
90. Santos AF, Douiri A, Becares N, Wu SY, Stephens A, Radulovic S, et al. Basophil activation test discriminates between allergy and tolerance in peanut-sensitized children. J Allergy Clin Immunol 2014;134:645-52. https://pubmed.ncbi.nlm.nih.gov/25065721/
91. Food Allergy Science Initiative, Broad Institute, MIT and Harvard University https://www.broadinstitute.org/scientific-areas/food-allergy-science-initiative
92. Al-Kouba J, Wilkinson AN, Starkey MR, Rudraraju R, Werder RB, Liu X et al. Allergen-encoding bone marrow transfer inactivates allergic T cell responses, alleviating airway inflammation. JCI Insight. 2017;2(11):e85742. https://insight.jci.org/articles/view/85742
93. Dr Manel Jordana, "Preventing Anaphylaxis in those with Food Allergy: Is it possible?", Webinar, Food Allergy Canada. 4 May 2021. https://foodallergycanada.ca/event/preventing-anaphylaxis-in-those-with-food-allergy-is-it-possible/
94. Ashley SE, "Working towards a safer and more effective oral immunotherapy – a treatment for food allergy", EAACI Patients. https://patients.eaaci.org/working-towards-a-safer-and-more-effective-oral-immunotherapy-a-treatment-for-food-allergy/
95. "Epinephrine Nasal Spray Demonstrates Bioequivalent Exposure and Absorption Rate Compared to Epinephrine Injectors", American Academy of Allergy and Clinical Immunology, https://www.aaaai.org/About/News/News/epinephrines
96. Kari Nadeau and Sloan Barnett, *The End of Food Allergy* (Vermilion, 2020)

FURTHER READING

97. Blood Test: Immunoglobulins https://kidshealth.org/en/parents/test-immunoglobulins.html
98. Immunoglobulins Michigan Medicine https://www.uofmhealth.org/health-library/hw41342
99. NCI Dictionary of Cancer Terms - Mast Cell https://www.cancer.gov/publications/dictionaries/cancer-terms/def/mast-cell
100. Scott-Taylor TH, O'B Hourihane J, Strobel S. Correlation of allergen-specific IgG subclass antibodies and T lymphocyte cytokine responses in children with multiple food allergies. Pediatr Allergy Immunol. 2010 Sep;21(6):935-44 https://pubmed.ncbi.nlm.nih.gov/20444160/
101. "Histamine: The Stuff Allergies are Made Of", MedlinePlus, September 8, 2017, https://medlineplus.gov/medlineplus-videos/histamine-the-stuff-allergies-are-made-of/

ABOUT THE AUTHOR

Goldie Putrym loves solving puzzles. Ever since her first child was diagnosed with severe eczema and life-threatening food allergies, deciphering the complex conditions has been her passion. Although she has worked with the European Space Agency and reported live on the European sovereign debt crisis, she finds the most gratification from helping people understand science and medicine.

She has an MA in journalism from City University London that has trained her to ask the right questions and delve deep into issues, and an MEng in aeronautical engineering from Imperial College that helps her take a multidisciplinary approach to solving problems.

A true global citizen and polyglot, she has lived in Asia, Europe and North America. She currently resides in London, England, with her husband and two children.

Printed in Great Britain
by Amazon

70299574R00081